ENGLISH ACCENTS
AND DIALECTS

ENGLISH ACCENTS AND DIALECTS

An introduction to social and regional varieties of
English in the British Isles

Fourth Edition

Arthur Hughes Peter Trudgill Dominic Watt

Hodder Arnold

A MEMBER OF THE HODDER HEADLINE GROUP

First published in Great Britain 1979
This edition published in Great Britain 2005 by
Hodder Education, a member of the Hodder Headline Group,
338 Euston Road, London NW1 3BH

www.hoddereducation.com

Distributed in the United States of America by
Oxford University Press Inc.
198 Madison Avenue, New York, NY10016

British Library Cataloguing in Publication Data
A catalogue record for this book is available from the British Library

Library of Congress Cataloging-in-Publication Data
A catalog record for this book is available from the Library of Congress

ISBN-10: 0340 88718 4
ISBN-13: 978 0 340 88718 9

1 2 3 4 5 6 7 8 9 10

This book is accompanied by a recording, which is available on CD only.

Typeset in 10 on 12pt Baskerville Book by
Phoenix Photosetting, Lordswood, Chatham, Kent
Printed and bound in Malta

What do you think about this book? Or any other Hodder Education title?
Please send your comments to the feedback section on www.hoddereducation.co.uk.

Contents

Acknowledgements

Third edition

A very large number of people have helped us with this book, and we can acknowledge only some of them here. Over the years we have profited enormously from discussions on varieties of English with Gerry Knowles and John Wells, and we are also very grateful to Peter Bedells, Viv Edwards, Sandra Foldvik, Erik Fudge, Vicky Hughes, Sandy Hutcheson, Elspeth Jones, Robin McClelland, Suzanne McClelland, James Milroy, Lesley Milroy, K.M. Petyt, and David Sutcliffe, who have provided us with information on specific points (sometimes without realizing it) and have corrected some of our worst misapprehensions. We would also like to thank all those people, many of whom went to a very great deal of trouble on our behalf, and some of whom prefer to remain anonymous, who helped us with the tape recordings. We would particularly like to acknowledge the assistance in this respect of Margaret Ainsbury, Tony Beard, Gillian Brown, Ray Brown, Edwin Cannon, Joy Cannon, Chris Connor, Roseanne Cook, Karen Currie, Fergus Daly, Sally Davies, Geoffrey Dearson, Angela Edmondson, Kirsty Evans, Anne Fenwick, Stanley Fletcher, Milton Greenwood, Isabel Holmes, David Holmes, Kathy Holmes, Carl James, Daisy James, Toni Johnson, Wilf Jones, Paul Kerswill, Gillian Lane-Plescia, Chris Lawrence, Catherine Lovell, Gillian Lovell, Caroline Macafee, Bridie McBride, Helen Mattacott, Jackie Mountford, Grahame Newell, Kristyan Spelman Miller, Enid Warnes, Gwyn Williams and, especially, Euan Reid. And, finally, we are very grateful indeed to R.W.P. Brasington, Jack Chambers, Paul Fletcher, Michael Garman, Hanne Svane Nielsen, and F. R. Palmer, who read earlier versions of the book and made many valuable suggestions for improvement.

Fourth edition

For assistance with the preparation of the fourth edition of *English Accents and Dialects* we are indebted to Brendan Cassidy, Deborah Clegg, Michael Deans, Susan Dunsmore, Bronwen Evans, Fidelma Farley, Carmen Llamas,

Mary O'Malley-Madec, Eva Martinez, Valery Moir, Shane Murphy, Anna-Maija Rist, Julie Robertson, Lucy Schiavone, Pam Thomson, Roderick Walters, George Watson, and Victoria Watt. Special thanks are due to Craig Lee for his assistance in the preparation of the maps and other illustrations.

THE INTERNATIONAL PHONETIC ALPHABET (revised to 1993, updated 1996)

CONSONANTS (PULMONIC)

	Bilabial	Labiodental	Dental	Alveolar	Postalveolar	Retroflex	Palatal	Velar	Uvular	Pharyngeal	Glottal
Plosive	p b			t d		ʈ ɖ	c ɟ	k ɡ	q ɢ		ʔ
Nasal	m	ɱ		n		ɳ	ɲ	ŋ	N		
Trill	ʙ			r					R		
Tap or Flap				ɾ		ɽ					
Fricative	ɸ β	f v	θ ð	s z	ʃ ʒ	ʂ ʐ	ç ʝ	x ɣ	χ ʁ	ħ ʕ	h ɦ
Lateral fricative				ɬ ɮ							
Approximant		ʋ		ɹ		ɻ	j	ɰ			
Lateral approximant				l		ɭ	ʎ	L			

Where symbols appear in pairs, the one to the right represents a voiced consonant. Shaded areas denote articulations judged impossible.

CONSONANTS (NON-PULMONIC)

Clicks		Voiced implosives		Ejectives	
ʘ	Bilabial	ɓ	Bilabial	ʼ	Examples:
ǀ	Dental	ɗ	Dental/alveolar	pʼ	Bilabial
ǃ	(Post)alveolar	ʄ	Palatal	tʼ	Dental/alveolar
ǂ	Palatoalveolar	ɠ	Velar	kʼ	Velar
ǁ	Alveolar lateral	ʛ	Uvular	sʼ	Alveolar fricative

OTHER SYMBOLS

ʍ	Voiceless labial-velar fricative	ɕ ʑ	Alveolo-palatal fricatives
w	Voiced labial-velar approximant	ɺ	Alveolar lateral flap
ɥ	Voiced labial-palatal approximant	ɧ	Simultaneous ʃ and x
ʜ	Voiceless epiglottal fricative		
ʢ	Voiced epiglottal fricative		Affricates and double articulations can be represented by two symbols joined by a tie bar if necessary.
ʡ	Epiglottal plosive		k͡p t͡s

VOWELS

Where symbols appear in pairs, the one to the right represents a rounded vowel.

SUPRASEGMENTALS

ˈ	Primary stress	ˌfoʊnəˈtɪʃən
ˌ	Secondary stress	
ː	Long	eː
ˑ	Half-long	eˑ
̆	Extra-short	ĕ
ǀ	Minor (foot) group	
‖	Major (intonation) group	
.	Syllable break	ɹi.ækt
‿	Linking (absence of a break)	

DIACRITICS

Diacritics may be placed above a symbol with a descender, e.g. ŋ̊

̥ Voiceless	n̥ d̥	̤ Breathy voiced	b̤ a̤	̪ Dental	t̪ d̪
̬ Voiced	s̬ t̬	̰ Creaky voiced	b̰ a̰	̺ Apical	t̺ d̺
ʰ Aspirated	tʰ dʰ	̼ Linguolabial	t̼ d̼	̻ Laminal	t̻ d̻
̹ More rounded	ɔ̹	ʷ Labialized	tʷ dʷ	̃ Nasalized	ẽ
̜ Less rounded	ɔ̜	ʲ Palatalized	tʲ dʲ	ⁿ Nasal release	dⁿ
̟ Advanced	u̟	ˠ Velarized	tˠ dˠ	ˡ Lateral release	dˡ
̠ Retracted	e̠	ˤ Pharyngealized	tˤ dˤ	̚ No audible release	d̚
̈ Centralized	ë	̴ Velarized or pharyngealized	ɫ		
̽ Mid-centralized	e̽	̝ Raised	e̝	(ɹ̝ = voiced alveolar fricative)	
̩ Syllabic	n̩	̞ Lowered	e̞	(β̞ = voiced bilabial approximant)	
̯ Non-syllabic	e̯	̘ Advanced Tongue Root	e̘		
˞ Rhoticity	ɚ a˞	̙ Retracted Tongue Root	e̙		

TONES AND WORD ACCENTS

LEVEL			CONTOUR		
e̋ or ꜒	Extra high		ě or ꜌		Rising
é ꜒	High		ê ꜜ		Falling
ē ꜓	Mid		e᷄ ꜓		High rising
è ꜕	Low		e᷅ ꜖		Low rising
ȅ ꜖	Extra low		e᷈ ꜔		Rising-falling
ꜜ	Downstep		↗		Global rise
ꜛ	Upstep		↘		Global fall

Word list

Words used in the recordings (shown here with RP pronunciation)

1 *pit* /pɪt/	**14** *beer* /bɪə/	**27** *pull* /pʊl/	**40** *plate* /pleɪt/
2 *pet* /pɛt/	**15** *bear* /bɛə/	**28** *pool* /puːl/	**41** *weight* /weɪt/
3 *pat* /pat/	**16** *bird* /bɜːd/	**29** *pole* /pəʊl/	**42** *poor* /pʊə/
4 *put* /pʊt/	**17** *bard* /bɑːd/	**30** *Paul* /pɔːl/	**43** *pour* /pɔː/
5 *putt* /pʌt/	**18** *board* /bɔːd/	**31** *doll* /dɒl/	**44** *pore* /pɔː/
6 *pot* /pɒt/	**19** *city* /sɪti/	**32** *cot* /kɒt/	**45** *paw* /pɔː/
7 *bee* /biː/	**20** *seedy* /siːdi/	**33** *caught* /kɔːt/	**46** *tide* /taɪd/
8 *bay* /beɪ/	**21** *hat* /hat/	**34** *fir* /fɜː/	**47** *tied* /taɪd/
9 *buy* /baɪ/	**22** *dance* /dɑːns/	**35** *fern* /fɜːn/	**48** *pause* /pɔːz/
10 *boy* /bɔɪ/	**23** *daft* /dɑːft/	**36** *fur* /fɜː/	**49** *paws* /pɔːz/
11 *boot* /buːt/	**24** *half* /hɑːf/	**37** *fair* /fɛə/	**50** *meet* /miːt/
12 *boat* /bəʊt/	**25** *father* /fɑːðə/	**38** *nose* /nəʊz/	**51** *meat* /miːt/
13 *bout* /baʊt/	**26** *farther* /fɑːðə/	**39** *knows* /nəʊz/	**52** *mate* /meɪt/

Note that the reader of the RP word list, as is typical of young to middle-aged speakers of the accent, has /bɛː/ for *bear* and /pɔː/ for *poor*.

CD track listing

Copyright statement (track 01)

Track no.	Contents	Track no.	Contents
02	RP word list	25	Aberdeen
03	RP speaker 1	26	Belfast word list
04	RP speaker 2	27	Belfast
05	RP speaker 3	28	Dublin word list
06	London word list	29	Dublin
07	London	30	Galway word list
08	Norwich word list	31	Galway
09	Norwich	32	Devon
10	Bristol word list	33	Northumberland
11	Bristol	34	Lowland Scots
12	Pontypridd word list	35	Test passage 1
13	Pontypridd	36	Test passage 2
14	Walsall word list	37	Test passage 3
15	Walsall	38	Test passage 4
16	Leicester word list	39	Test passage 5
17	Leicester	40	Test passage 6
18	Bradford word list	41	Test passage 7
19	Bradford	42	Test passage 8
20	Liverpool word list	43	Test passage 9
21	Liverpool	44	Test passage 10
22	Edinburgh word list	45	Test passage 11
23	Edinburgh	46	Test passage 12
24	Aberdeen word list	47	Test passage 13

1 Variation in English

When foreign learners of English first come to the British Isles, they are usually surprised (and dismayed) to discover how little they understand of the English they hear. For one thing, people seem to speak faster than expected. Also, the English that most British or Irish people speak seems to be different in many ways from the English the visitor has learned. While it is probably differences of pronunciation that will immediately strike them, learners may also notice differences of grammar and vocabulary.

Their reactions to this experience will vary. If they are confident in their own ability and that of their teacher(s), they may conclude that most of the English, Welsh, Scottish, and Irish people that they hear do not – or even cannot – speak English correctly. In this they would find that many native speakers agree with them. They might even be told that, since foreign learners have usually studied English in a formal way, they should know better than would native speakers what is correct.

We can deal in two ways with the suggestion that native speakers cannot speak their own language correctly. Firstly, for learners visiting the British Isles the question of correctness is largely irrelevant. Their problem is to understand what they hear, regardless of whether it is 'correct' or not. The description and analysis of variation provided in this book, together with the recordings on the compact disk, are attempts to help them to do this. This information should also help them decide which features of what they hear they can safely integrate into their own speech. The second thing we can do is to try to show that the notion of correctness is not really useful or appropriate when describing the language of native speakers. We will not do this immediately, but will raise the issue later in the book, when examples of what might be considered 'incorrect' English are discussed.

Another reaction on the part of learners who fail to understand what is being said may be to think that perhaps what they learned in their own country was not 'real' English. Fortunately, this is increasingly unlikely to be the case. Although the English they have learned is real enough, however, it will tend to be limited to a single variety of the language, a variety chosen to serve as a model for their own speech. It will usually be the speech variety of a particular group of native speakers as that variety is spoken, slowly and carefully, in relatively formal situations. Given limitations of time, of teachers' knowledge, and of students' aspirations and attitudes, this restriction is entirely reasonable, at least as far as speaking is concerned. Though learners may sound a little odd at times, they will usually be able to make themselves understood. But such a restriction as far as listening comprehension is concerned is less easily justified. While native speakers may be able to 'decode' the learners' messages, they generally have neither the ability nor the inclination to 'encode' their own messages in a form more comprehensible to learners. In many cases, of course, native speakers will simply not be aware of such difficulties. Even when they are, a common strategy is to repeat what has just been said, only louder, or to revert to 'foreigner talk' (me come, you go – OK?), usually making understanding even more difficult. It seems to us, then, that exposure to a number of varieties of English, and help in understanding them, can play an important and practically useful part in the study of English as a foreign language.

Even when learners with comprehension problems recognize that English, like their own language – indeed, like every language – is subject to variation, that variation can be so complex and at times so subtle that it is usually a long time before they begin to see much order in it. And native speakers, even those who teach the language, are often hard put to explain the things that puzzle learners. For this reason, we will attempt now to give some idea of the principal ways in which British and Irish English speech varies and, just as importantly, the non-linguistic (social, geographical) factors which condition that variation. It is hoped by doing this to provide a framework within which to set the features of social and regional variation, which will be our main concern in the remainder of the book.

Variation in pronunciation

RP

We should first make clear the way we are going to use two important terms, **dialect** and **accent**. We use dialect to refer to varieties distinguished from each other by differences of grammar and vocabulary. Accent, on the other hand, refers to variations in pronunciation. The reason for making this distinction will become clear as the chapter progresses.

Whenever British rather than, say, American English is taught to overseas or foreign learners, the accent presented as a model for the learner will most typically be **received pronunciation**, abbreviated RP. 'Received' here is to be understood in its nineteenth-century sense of 'accepted in the most polite circles of society'. While British society has changed a good deal since that time, RP has – at least in England – nevertheless remained the accent of those in the upper reaches of the social scale, as measured by education, income and profession, or title. It has traditionally been the accent of those educated at public schools (which in the UK are of course private, and beyond the means of most parents), and it is largely through these schools, and state schools aspiring to emulate them, that the accent has been perpetuated. RP, unlike prestige accents in other countries, is not the accent of any particular region, except historically: its origins were in the speech of London and the surrounding area. It has often been contended that it is, at least in principle, impossible to tell from his or her pronunciation alone where an RP speaker comes from (though see Trudgill 2002). As suggested above, RP has greatest currency and enjoys the highest prestige in England, and is evaluated somewhat differently in the other countries of the UK and in Ireland (in Scotland it is considered very much to be an 'English' accent, for instance, and its speakers are not necessarily always accorded greater respect than are speakers of other accents; for further discussion of the varying prestige of RP, see Milroy 2001).

It has been estimated that only about 3 to 5 per cent of the population of England speaks RP (see Trudgill 2002: 171–2). Since it is clearly a minority accent, why, then, is it by and large the only British accent taught to foreign learners? Its high prestige has already been mentioned. No doubt learners want to learn, and teachers to teach, what has long been perceived to be the 'best' accent. Among a substantial proportion of British people, because they tend to associate the accent with the high social status, wealth and power of its speakers, RP is usually considered the best, the clearest, and even the most 'beautiful' accent. There is another reason, however, for learning RP. If we were asked to point to a readily available example of RP, we would probably suggest the speech of some BBC newsreaders. Because of its use on radio and television, within Britain RP has become probably the most widely understood of all accents. This in turn means that the learner who succeeds in speaking it, other things being equal, has the best chance of being understood wherever he or she goes in the British Isles. Another good reason for learning RP is that it is by far the most thoroughly described of British accents. This is the case, at least in part, because descriptions of it were made in response to the needs of foreign learners and their teachers. We describe the sounds of RP in Chapter 3.

Language change

Learners who have been presented with RP as a model should not think, when they come to Britain, that speech they hear which is in some way different from that model is necessarily not RP. First, accents, like all components of living languages, change with time. In RP, for example, there has for some considerable time been a tendency, through a process known by linguists as **smoothing**, for certain triphthongs (vowels with three distinct qualities) and diphthongs (two qualities) to become monophthongs (so-called 'pure' vowels with a single quality). Thus the word *tyre*, which was once most commonly pronounced /taɪə/ (with a triphthong), came to be pronounced /tɑə/ (with a diphthong), and is now increasingly reduced to /tɑː/ (with a monophthong, such that it has the same pronunciation as the word *tar*). This smoothing to [ɑː] can also be observed in the traditional RP triphthong /aʊə/, as in *tower* or *hour*. Thus Major-General Patrick Cordingley, commenting on BBC radio during the 2003 Iraq conflict, talked repeatedly of 'Allied [fɑːpɑː]' (*firepower*).

Smoothing of these vowels appears to be most common among younger RP speakers, but there is of course not a perfect correlation between age and pronunciation. Some RP speakers, including younger ones, will regard the distinguishing features of the advanced variety of the accent (see p. 41) as 'affected' and will not alter their own speech, at least not until the adoption of these features becomes more general with the passage of time. Other RP speakers will be only too ready to integrate them into their own speech. We might see some speakers, accordingly, as 'early adopters', and others as 'conservative'. For this reason, it would be misleading to say there is only one, fixed form of the accent, since at any stage the accent will be a mixture of traditional and innovative features (see further Fabricius 2002; Trudgill 2002).

Which variety of RP is taught will differ from country to country, even from classroom to classroom. What learners of advanced RP should bear in mind is that this form of pronunciation does sound affected to most British people, even in England, and that, if the learner acquires it successfully, he or she may still be thought to sound affected even though listeners may be aware that they are listening to a foreigner. For many people with regional accents, all RP speech, however conservative, sounds affected, and it is probably true to say that the supposed affectation is perceived most strongly in places where the differences between RP and the regional accent of the listener are most marked.

This long-standing association of RP with affectation, social snobbery, aloofness, and so on, is increasingly out of keeping with the kind of image many of the accent's younger speakers would wish to project of themselves. This trend has not gone unnoticed by the media. Since the third edition of this book was published, ever larger quantities of column space and air time have been devoted to what has been termed the 'dumbing down' of the spoken and written English used by young British people. Specifically, the influence of non-standard and foreign accents and dialects of English, along with a general deterioration in standards in other modes of behaviour (dress, manners, respect for elders, etc.), has been blamed for the perceived rise of 'sloppiness' in pronunciation and disregard for 'proper grammar'. Many media pundits have become so convinced of the decline of RP and Standard English that the emergence of a new replacement variety first dubbed 'Estuary English' by Rosewarne (1984) has been accepted almost universally, in spite of the fact that the existence and separate identity of this 'new' variety are argued for on the basis of rather little reliable linguistic evidence (see Trudgill 2002: 177–9).

The usual definition of Estuary English is that it is a compromise between or amalgam of RP and working-class London speech (Cockney), and is thus a 'neutral' variety which simultaneously provides the opportunity for lower-class speakers to appear higher status than they are, and for middle- and upper-class speakers to appear lower status than they are, in keeping with the social levelling claimed to have been a key characteristic of life in the United Kingdom in recent decades. The use of 'Estuary' forms by people from privileged or affluent backgrounds, however, is not without its pitfalls, if we can judge by the adverse reactions in the British press to the use of such forms by the prime minister, Tony Blair, and certain members of the royal family. A particularly salient, widely discussed and often heavily stigmatized 'Estuary' form is glottal stop [ʔ] as a pronunciation of /t/ in certain contexts; this is discussed further on pp. 42–3 and p. 54.

Another example of a feature entering modern RP which probably has its origins in a non-standard accent is the [w]-like labio-dental approximant [ʋ] (as a pronunciation of /ɹ/) that appears to be spreading fairly fast in British English. While RP speakers of any age can be heard to produce words like *road, brown, very*, etc. using this pronunciation of /ɹ/, it is much less unusual to hear it used in the speech of young RP speakers than in that of older ones. If it is noticed at all, it is certainly regarded as a much less idiosyncratic or 'disordered' feature of an individual RP speaker than was the case even a generation ago, and is a good less stigmatized as a result. In most parts of England, it would be true to say that the use of [ʋ] is no longer regarded by schoolteachers and speech therapists as a 'speech impediment' as it once was, except perhaps where it occurred in upper-class speech, in which it seems to have been tolerated as a foppish affectation. As the stigma of [ʋ] recedes, then, so its adoption by a new generation of speakers is all the more likely. The possibility has been raised (see Foulkes and Docherty 2000) that the labio-dental pronunciation, which is common in infantile speech, owes its current spread to the relaxation of the stigma of 'childishness' associated with it. That is, children no longer learn to stop using the 'childish' [ʋ] pronunciation when they reach adolescence and adulthood, because the social pressure to switch to a more 'adult' pronunciation has been removed.

Another example of a change which is still at a relatively early stage in its progress is the so-called variously **high-rising tone**, the **high rise terminal** (HRT), **Australian Question Intonation** (AQI) or 'uptalk' (see Cruttenden 1995, 1997; Bauer 2002). This phenomenon is often defined as the use, in statements, of the rising intonation pattern normally associated with questions (in RP, at any rate; other accents of British English, such as those of Glasgow or Belfast, have quite different statement and question intonation patterns from those used in RP; see Chapter 5). For this reason, some commentators – usually opinionated but underinformed journalists rather than linguists – interpret high-rising tone as an indication of general uncertainty and lack of confidence on the part of the young people who use it. These commentators tend to attribute its appearance to the influence – either through face-to-face interaction, or passively through television viewing – of Australian and New Zealand English, both of which share this property. The interesting suggestion has also been raised that the pattern has entered British English because it has become so common for young British school-leavers to travel independently overseas on the 'backpacking trail', often for extended periods. While so doing they are likely – even if they do not actually visit Australia or New Zealand – to encounter large numbers of independent travellers from the southern hemisphere, and may travel in areas in which they must frequently interact with local people whose command of English is not always very good. It is commonly observed that in the latter situation native English speakers have a tendency to raise the pitch towards the end of utterances more frequently than they would when talking to other native speakers, as a means of checking that their utterances are being understood. In these circumstances, then, the use of high-rising tone may have come to act as a badge of 'well-travelled' or 'worldly' status. In tandem with its association with the appealing stereotype of Australians and New Zealanders as relaxed, friendly, open, sporty, fun-loving (etc.), it might therefore be unsurprising that the feature would be imported into British accents, later to spread among children, adolescents and young adults with no direct experience of independent foreign travel or contact with people from the southern hemisphere.

The full picture is, however, certainly more complex than this, not least because high-rising tone patterns are not altogether like the question intonation patterns used by the same speakers. The claim that the use of HRT patterns indicates 'uncertainty' is also probably untenable, given that such patterns may be used when giving information about which the speaker cannot have any doubt (e.g. when telling someone his or her name and address). And, of course, any similarity to southern hemisphere intonation patterns may be nothing more than coincidence.

Patterns of this sort have been used in American English for several decades, for instance, and American English may equally well be the source of HRT in British English. For further discussion, see Foulkes and Docherty (2005) or, for a more technical treatment of these phenomena, Fletcher, Grabe and Warren (2005).

Stylistic variation

As we have seen, then, there are differences of pronunciation among RP speakers. There is, in addition, variation in the pronunciation of individual RP speakers. It is perhaps trivial, but is nonetheless true, that studies in instrumental phonetics have shown that a person cannot produce even a single speech sound in exactly the same way twice in succession. And it is obvious that people with food in their mouths, with heavy colds, or who have just drunk eight pints of beer, will not speak in quite the same way as in other circumstances. But what is more significant for us are the changes in pronunciation made, consciously or unconsciously, by speakers according to their perception of the situation in which they find themselves, especially how formal or informal they feel it to be. Their judgement of formality will depend on a number of factors, such as the relative status of the people they are talking to, how well they know each other, what they are talking about, to what purpose and in what place. Some idea of the range of formality can be given by listing just a few of the terms for occasions on which words are uttered – proclamation, lecture, consultation, conversation, chat. In what speakers see as a very formal situation they will tend to articulate more slowly and carefully. Individual sounds will be given, as it were, their 'full' value; fewer will be omitted (or **elided**, to use the technical term; **elision** is extremely common in all varieties of spoken English). In a very informal situation, on the other hand, speakers will be more likely to speak quickly, less carefully, and some sounds will either have their values changed or be elided altogether. Thus, say, for an RP speaker the word *are* may be pronounced /ɑː/ in deliberate speech, but (when **destressed**) will become /ə/ in more casual speech, this process being known as **vowel weakening**. In the phrase /ðat pleɪt/ *that plate* the final consonant of the first word will often become [p] through **assimilation** (becoming similar) to the first consonant of the second, such that the phrase is pronounced [ðap pleɪt], while /ɪk'spɛkt səʊ/ *expect so* may be pronounced ['spɛk səʊ] through elision of certain sounds. We refer to variation conditioned by speakers' perceptions of the situation in which they are speaking as **stylistic variation**.

It should not be thought that a more casual style of pronunciation is in any sense incorrect. It is really not a matter of correctness, but of appropriateness to the situation. It would be odd, even ridiculous, for a radio commentator to use the same style of pronunciation when telling his girlfriend how desirable she is, as when describing for his listeners a royal procession. It is just possible, nevertheless, that there are radio commentators who *would* do this, for it is not only situational factors which determine style of pronunciation, but also the speaker's personality. Some people are very sensitive to what they regard as the demands of a situation on their speech style, while others appear indifferent, speaking with little change of pronunciation in the widest range of situations. Some of those who always speak carefully and with great deliberation maintain that to do anything else is 'slovenly' or 'sloppy', and leads to loss of clarity and to possible misunderstanding. In this claim they forget how much of language is redundant: there is usually far more information packed into an utterance than we need in order to understand it. The small loss in information resulting from modifications in pronunciation of the kind exemplified above rarely causes confusion: ['spɛk səʊ] can only be *expect so*. Even where linguistically there is ambiguity, the situation will normally disambiguate what is meant. If we are asked if we would like some [mɪns], for example, we can infer without too much difficulty from the proffered rattling bag that the offer is of mints and not mince (i.e. minced meat). And if we are not sure, in an informal situation it would be perfectly natural to ask which was intended.

As we said earlier, whatever learners think about this kind of thing, their task is essentially to understand what is said. Unfortunately, it is a task they are not always well prepared for. Language teachers, like all of us, want to be understood, and are inclined to speak slowly and with deliberation, a tendency in which they are not discouraged either by their students or by the often quite formal atmosphere of the classroom. Learners may be familiar with such processes as vowel weakening, assimilation and elision, but they usually have little idea of the degree to which these occur in ordinary conversational English. Even the recorded conversations of native speakers marketed commercially can sound rather stiff and stilted. In response to this, there are many recordings available these days which sound more naturalistic and spontaneous, including those on the CD accompanying this book (also Foulkes and Docherty 1999, and numerous recordings available for download from the internet; see *Further Reading*).

Unconditioned variation

Within RP there are differences of pronunciation which cannot be explained in terms either of change over time or of speech style. An example of such a variable form is the pronunciation of *economic* as /iːkə'nɒmɪk/ or /ɛkə'nɒmɪk/. Speakers will have an individual preference for one over the other, and – at least until it is demonstrated that there is some reason for this preference – the best we can say is that some people, perhaps a majority, use this pronunciation, and other people use the other pronunciation. This kind of variation is known as **free variation**.

Regional variation

As we have seen, only a very small percentage of the population of England speak RP, meaning that in the British Isles as a whole the proportion of RP speakers is very small indeed. The rest of the islands' native English-speaking inhabitants have some form of regional accent. Much of Chapters 4 and 5 is concerned with regional accents, and we shall do no more here than make some general observations.

Regional accents are sometimes spoken of as, for instance, 'northern' or 'southern' English, 'Irish', or 'Welsh'. But this is not to say that there is, for example, one Irish or one north of England accent. It means only that speakers in one of those areas – say, Wales – have enough pronunciation features in common with each other which are not shared with speakers from other areas, for us to say of someone we hear speaking, 'He's from Wales.' And just as 'northern accent' is no more than a convenient label for a group of more local accents, a label like 'Yorkshire accent' is simply a label for a group of accents which are more local still. Almost no matter how small an area we look at, we will find differences between the pronunciation there and an area adjoining it. At the same time, unless there is some considerable obstacle to communication between the two areas, such as a mountain range, a large river estuary, or a stretch of sea or ocean, those differences will be so slight that we would be unhappy about drawing a line between them and saying that on one side of the line the accent is X and on the other it is Y. In Britain, from the south-west of England to the north of Scotland, we do not have a succession of distinct accents, but an **accent continuum**, a gradual changing of pronunciation. In order to describe regional variation, however, it is convenient at times to speak of accents as if they were entities to be found within certain defined limits, and from here on this is what we will do.

Speakers of RP tend to be found at the top of the social scale, and their speech gives no clue to their regional origin. People at the bottom of the social scale speak with the most obvious, the 'broadest', regional accents. Between these two extremes, in general (and there are always individual exceptions) the higher a person is on the social scale, the less regionally marked will be his or her accent, and the less it is likely to differ from RP. This relationship between class and accent can be represented diagrammatically in the form of a triangle, as in Figure 1.1.

This relationship between accent and the social scale can be illustrated with figures for 'H-dropping' (for example, where *hat* is pronounced /at/

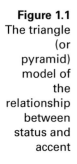

Figure 1.1
The triangle (or pyramid) model of the relationship between status and accent

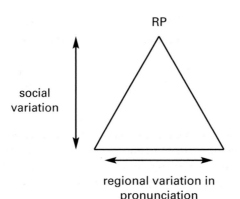

Table 1.1
H-dropping in Bradford, West Yorkshire (from Petyt 1977)

	% H-dropping
Upper middle class	12
Lower middle class	28
Upper working class	67
Middle working class	89
Lower working class	93

instead of /hat/) in the Bradford area of West Yorkshire (Petyt 1977), as shown in Table 1.1.

Not all people stay in one social position throughout their lives. In England, there has been a tendency for those climbing the social scale to modify their accent in the direction of RP, thereby helping to maintain the relationship between class and accent. In the case of speakers with Bradford accents, this would involve starting to pronounce /h/ at the start of words like *hat*, *happen* and *horrible* more often than they did before. They might also try to introduce the vowel /ʌ/, which is absent from northern English accents but which in RP distinguishes *putt* /pʌt/ from *put* /pʊt/ (this distinction is in fact found in practically all accents of English beyond England). But to do this is not easy. It means dividing all those words which in the north of England contain the vowel /ʊ/, like *put*, *bush*, *pudding*, *cup*, *bus*, *shut*, etc., into two groups according to their pronunciation in RP. What often happens is that some words which have /ʊ/ in RP as well as in the regional accent are wrongly classified, and so the northern English would-be RP-speaker pronounces *cushion* as /ˈkʌʃn̩/, such that it rhymes with (RP) *Russian* /ˈɹʌʃn̩/. This kind of misassignation of certain pronunciations is referred to as **hypercorrection** (see p. 60).

There is, however, not the same pressure as there once was to modify one's speech in the direction of RP. Newsreaders and announcers with non-RP accents are now commonplace on the BBC – once a bastion of the most elevated and conservative form of the accent – and in other spheres of public life, such as politics, academia, or the civil service, there is no longer any expectation that RP accents will be used to the exclusion of virtually any others. It is really only in the highest echelons of British society, in the English public schools, and in the officer classes of the military, that earlier attitudes towards RP are maintained. Among the general public, RP is still highly valued in the sense that it is equated with being 'well-spoken' or 'articulate', and is perceived widely as a signal of general intelligence and competence, but it is no longer considered essential for certain occupations. We can gain an appreciation for how attitudes have changed when we examine the results of two similar experiments carried out around 30 years apart.

In the original experiment, which was carried out by Howard Giles and his colleagues in South Wales in the 1970s, a university lecturer, who was introduced as such, gave the same talk, word for word, to two matched groups of schoolchildren aged 16 to 18 years (Giles *et al.* 1975). The only difference between the two talks was the accent used. The lecturer addressed one group in RP, the other in a Birmingham accent. When the schoolchildren were then asked to evaluate the lecturer according to a number of criteria, those who had heard him speak RP gave him a significantly higher rating of intelligence than the group who had heard him use a Birmingham accent.

More recently, the results of a replication study of Giles (1970) carried out by Sarah Wood (reported in Stockwell 2002) show that RP was still judged by a panel of young female students to be a sign of higher-than-average intelligence, but also that an RP accent did not indicate higher social status than did west London and Norwich accents. RP was also judged 'less pleasing' than these accents. The implications are, therefore, that despite its continuing association with intelligence (and competence), an RP accent no longer has the 'statusfulness' or 'attractiveness' that it did a generation ago.

Grammatical and lexical variation

Standard English

The term accent, as we have seen, refers to varieties of pronunciation. The term dialect, on the other hand (at least as we shall use it here) refers to varieties distinguished from each other by differences of grammar (**morphology** and **syntax**) and vocabulary (**lexis**). With British English, though not with all other languages, the separation of accent from dialect is not only logically possible, but is almost required by the relationship that holds between them. The accent taught to most foreign learners of British English is RP. The dialect used as a model is known as 'Standard English', which is the dialect of educated people throughout the British Isles. It is the dialect normally used in writing, for teaching in schools and universities, and the one most often heard on radio and television. Unlike RP, Standard English is *not* restricted to the speech of a particular social group. While it would be odd to hear an RP speaker consistently using a non-standard dialect of English, most users of Standard English have regional accents. What social variation there is within Standard English appears to be limited to a rather small number of lexical items. The choice of the word *serviette* rather than (table) *napkin*, for example, has been said to indicate inferior social standing.

Another way in which Standard English differs from RP is that it exhibits significant regional variation. Subsumed under Standard English (or Standard British English) are Standard English English (in England and Wales), Standard Scottish English, and Standard Irish English. In Scotland and Ireland there are regional features which, because they are to be found regularly even in formal writing, are considered 'standard'. In Standard Scottish English, for example, we can find *They hadn't a good time* rather than the Standard English English *They didn't have a good time*, and forms such as *furth of* and *outwith*, both of which are equivalent to *outside* or *beyond*. It is of course almost always the Standard English English forms which are taught to foreign students, even in Scotland. Variation between these standard dialects is in fact quite limited, and should cause learners few problems.

Language change

The grammar of a dialect changes with time, but very slowly. Grammatical forms and structures, members of tightly knit, closed systems, resist alteration, and it is not always easy to identify ongoing grammatical development.

One interesting example of grammatical variation which may represent the beginning of a change in the language is the apparently increasing use of the **present perfect** construction in conjunction with expressions of definite past time reference. We may hear utterances such as *And Roberts has played for us last season* (implying that he did so without any kind of break). Most native speakers, it must be admitted, would find this odd. They would claim that the speaker had made a mistake. But sentences like this are heard more and more often. The captain of a cricket team who said *And Roberts has played for us last season* had been asked about the present strength of his side. His answer combined an indication of the current relevance of Roberts' having played with the information that it was in the previous season that he had played. In this way he said in one sentence what can normally only be said in two: *Roberts has played for us. He played last season.* It is not at all certain that the use of this grammatical device will continue to increase. For the time being it will be regarded as a mistake, or at any rate rather odd-sounding. But if eventually it becomes generally accepted (just as previously 'incorrect' sentences like *The house is being built next spring* are now accepted as good English), then it will be yet another subtlety for foreign learners to master, in an area which is already difficult enough.

Lexical change is more rapid than grammatical change. It is easier to see the variation that sometimes accompanies it. In some cases a new lexical item enters the language and displaces one already there. In this way the word *radio* took the place of *wireless*, the latter of which (in the sense of *radio*) is now heard exclusively in the speech of the elderly, although it can be heard in computing- and electronics-related phrases such as *wireless Europe, wireless communications, wireless microphone*, etc.

In other cases, an established lexical item begins to change its meaning, or take on a second meaning. The word *aggravate*, for instance, which not long ago exclusively meant 'make worse' (as in the phrases *Don't aggravate the situation* or *aggravated burglary*), is now probably more often used to mean something like 'irritate', as in *Hearing her talk about her latest foreign holiday is really aggravating.* There are some people – the kind who write tetchy letters to newspaper editors – who argue that since *aggravate* is derived from the Latin *aggravare*, which has the meaning 'make worse' or 'make heavier', then that must be the true meaning of *aggravate* in English. But if this argument were applied generally, it would suggest that the real meaning of *nice*, since it is derived from the Latin *nescius*, is 'ignorant'.

There are other people who argue that giving a second meaning to *aggravate* could lead to misunderstanding. This is hardly likely, as in its first sense the verb requires an abstract object, while in its second sense it requires an animate object. At present, many educated people continue to avoid using *aggravate* to mean 'irritate', at least in their written English. Foreign learners, while recognizing the possibility of a second meaning for *aggravate* (and for other words like *chronic, flaunt, infer* or *literally* that are also changing), should probably do the same.

Stylistic variation

The choice of grammatical structure and vocabulary will vary with the situation in which people are speaking. On a very formal occasion someone might say *the man to whom I wrote*, while less formally they might say *the bloke I wrote to*. One phrase is not more correct than the other, even if *bloke* might strike the reader as less formal than *man*. And despite the protestations of pedants, there is no reason, except custom and personal preference, why **prepositions** like *to* (and *from, into, above, up,* etc.) should not end sentences. Nor is there anything grammatically wrong with inserting an **adverb** such as *pointlessly* between the two parts of a **verb infinitive** like *to criticize* to create the phrase *to pointlessly criticize*. Objections to such so-called **split infinitives** in English originate in the pronouncement that since one cannot split verb infinitives in Latin in this way, the process should not be allowed to occur in English. It seems obvious to most of us, though, that what happened to be the case in Latin is not necessarily the case in English, and there is little sense in trying to transfer grammatical rules from a dead Romance language into a living Germanic one. Defenders of grammatical correctness in English predict that the decline in the teaching of 'rules' like 'Don't end sentences with prepositions' and 'Avoid splitting infinitives' will inevitably lead to some kind of linguistic free-for-all, where speakers will be able to flout the rules as they please, and pepper their speech with slang and swear words with impunity. But again, it should be remembered that swear words and slang are not intrinsically wrong in themselves: as with the features of pronunciation discussed earlier, it is a matter not of correctness, but of appropriateness to the situation.

When even highly educated people are chatting together with friends, their speech is very different in style from textbook conversation. This can be demonstrated very convincingly by recording a conversation and then transcribing it as precisely as possible, as we have done in later sections of this book. It is always surprising how much 'noise' there is in the spoken language people produce when their utterances are unplanned (in the sense of them improvising what they are saying, rather than repeating something memorized, or reading from a script). This is true even of speakers we think of as particularly fluent and articulate. It is quite normal for speakers to begin a sentence, then change their mind; they hesitate, then start again, differently; they use pause fillers like *er* and *um* with surprising frequency; they muddle one grammatical structure with another, and transpose words out of their normal order. They omit various words, forget others, replacing them with *thingy* or *wotsit*, and if necessary they will invent words (known as **nonce words**) just for the occasion. In a relaxed atmosphere they do not feel constrained to speak carefully or to plan what they are going to say. And in such casual speech situations speakers' utterances will overlap with each other a good deal.

This makes understanding difficult for learners, of course. But once account is taken of their difficulties and people begin to speak more slowly and carefully, inevitably the atmosphere changes somewhat.

Regional variation

Standard English, as we have said, is a dialect. Besides this, there are many regional dialects in Britain, which differ from Standard English in various ways. There are grammatical differences. So, in East Anglia the third person singular present tense is not marked with a final –*s*. We find *he go*, *he eat* instead of Standard English *he goes*, *he eats*. There are differences, too, of vocabulary. What is known as a *clothes horse* in Standard English and southern English dialects is called a *maiden* in northern English dialects.

Not everybody speaks the dialect of the area they belong to. There is a relationship between social class and dialect similar to the one between social class and accent. The higher a person's position on the social scale, the less regionally marked his or her speech is likely to be. This can be exemplified with the figures from a survey carried out in Norwich, in the East Anglian county of Norfolk (see Map 5.2 on p. 79). The number of third person singular present tense verb forms without –*s* was counted and then expressed as a percentage of all third person singular present tense verb forms. The results for various social groups were as follows (Trudgill 1974).

	% forms without -*s*
Upper middle class	0
Lower middle class	29
Upper working class	75
Middle working class	81
Lower working class	97

Table 1.2 Third person singular present tense verb forms without –*s* in Norwich (Trudgill 1974)

Until fairly recently, teachers in British schools made great efforts to eradicate features of local dialect from the speech and, more particularly, the writing of their pupils. Teachers were inclined to think of these regional features as mistakes in Standard English. They were, however, not very successful in their efforts. Today, teachers and educational policy-makers are a good deal more tolerant of regional and social variation in the language used by schoolchildren. It is true, nonetheless, that the longer children stay at school, and the more successful they are, the less regionally marked, grammatically and lexically, their speech is likely to be. But, as length of stay and success at school themselves correlate highly with social class, this may not be very significant. It is true, however, that some people do modify their speech quite considerably. In many cases they can be regarded as having two dialects, speaking Standard English in certain company and their local dialect (often with a more marked regional accent than they usually affect) in other company. In this way they make a claim to belong to more than one social group. Many young British people report that staying in education as far as university level has an additional standardizing effect on their English, such that while their English may be perceived by university acquaintances as regionally distinct, it is seen as somehow 'diluted' or 'posh' by their friends and family back home.

Correctness

We have mentioned the idea of correctness on a number of occasions already in this chapter. We want here just to summarize briefly what we have said. Three types of things are often said to be incorrect.

The first type is elements which are new to the language. Resistance to these by many speakers seems inevitable, but almost as inevitable, as long as these elements prove useful, is their eventual acceptance into the language. The learner needs to recognize these and understand them. It is interesting to note that resistance seems weakest to change in pronunciation. There are linguistic reasons for this but, in the case of the RP accent, the fact that innovation is introduced by the social elite must play a part.

The second type is features of informal speech. This, we have argued, is a matter of style, not correctness. It is like wearing clothes. Most people reading this book will see nothing wrong in wearing a bikini, but such an outfit would seem a little out of place in an office (no more out of place, however, than a business suit would be for lying on the beach). In the same way, there are words one would not normally use when making a speech at a conference which would be perfectly acceptable in bed, and vice versa.

The third type is features of regional speech. We have said little about correctness in relation to these, because we think that once they are recognized for what they are, and not thought debased or deviant forms of the prestige dialect or accent, the irrelevance of the notion of correctness will be obvious.

Summary

At present, the most prestigious British dialect is Standard English; the most prestigious accent is RP. It is with these that overseas learners are generally most familiar, assuming they are learning British English rather than American or Australian English. What they are not usually so familiar with, however, is the degree of variation to be found within

Standard English and RP. This variation, part of it stylistic, part of it attributable to changes in the language, is not the subject matter of this book, although we have included suggestions for further reading towards the end. Nevertheless, it is important that learners should be aware of the existence and effects of stylistic variation and variation over time, and not mistake it for the social and regional variation with which we are principally concerned.

Standard English is the dialect used by educated people throughout the British Isles. Nevertheless, most people in Britain and Ireland (including many who would generally be regarded as speakers of Standard English) have at least some regional dialect forms in their speech. In general, the higher people are on the social scale, the fewer of these regional forms their speech will exhibit. The main ways in which regional dialects differ from Standard English are outlined in the next chapter.

RP, lastly, is not the accent of any region. It is spoken by a very small percentage of the British population, those at the top of the social scale. Everyone else has a regional accent of some sort. The lower a person is on the social scale, the more obvious their regional accent will tend to be to listeners. Differences between RP and regional accents are discussed in Chapter 4.

2 Dialect variation

Variation within Standard English

The Standard English dialect itself is subject to a certain amount of variation. Some of this is regional: educated people in different parts of Britain do vary to a certain extent in the way in which they speak, and even write, English. (These differences normally involve features which are also found in the regional non-standard dialects.) And some of it is to do with age: as we saw in Chapter 1, all languages and dialects change, and Standard English is no exception.

1 **Speakers of Standard English in the south of England tend to use** *contracted negatives* **of the type:**

> *I haven't got it*
> *She won't go*
> *Doesn't he like it?*

The further north one goes, the more likely one is to hear the alternative type:

> *I've not got it*
> *She'll not go*
> *Does he not like it?*

This is particularly true of Derbyshire, Lancashire, Cumbria and Scotland. In Scotland, forms of this type are used particularly frequently. Elsewhere, it is more a matter of tendencies than of absolute rules. Southern English speakers (see above) use the northern-type contraction in *I'm not*, since *I amn't* does not occur in Standard English, although it does in other dialects, such as those spoken in Scotland. Southern English speakers also quite frequently use the *you're not ~ we're not ~ they're not* forms alongside the more typically southern-type forms with *aren't*. Part of the reason for this may lie in the stigmatized non-standard usage of this form with the first person singular, *I aren't*.

2   **In most grammatical descriptions of Standard English it is stated that the *indirect object* precedes the direct object:**

She gave the man a book
She gave him it
She gave him the book

If the preposition *to* is employed, however, then of course the direct object can precede the indirect object:

She gave a book to the man
She gave it to him
She gave a book to him
She gave it to the man

In the south of England, the forms with *to* seem to be the most common, particularly where the direct object is a **pronoun** like *him, her, it, them*, etc. However, in the educated speech of people from the north of England, other structures are also possible, as demonstrated in the following:

(a) *She gave it him* is very common indeed, and is also quite acceptable to many southern speakers.

(b) *She gave it the man* is also very common in the north of England, but is not found in the south.

(c) *She gave the book him* is not so common, but it can nonetheless be heard in the north of England, particularly if there is contrastive stress on *him*.

(d) *She gave a book the man* is not especially common, but it does occur in northern varieties, particularly again if *man* is contrastively stressed.

3   **There are regional differences in which *participle* forms are used after verbs such as *need* and *want*:**

Southern England	*I want it washed*
	It needs washing
Parts of midland and northern England	*I want it washing*
	It needs washing
Scotland	*I want it washed*
	It needs washed

4   **There are a number of regional and age-group differences in the use of the verbs *must* and *have to*. These can be demonstrated with reference to Table 2.1.**

Table 2.1
Must and *have to* in southern English English

		(a) positive	(b) negative modal	(c) negative main verb
non-epistemic	(1)	he must do it he has to do it he's got to do it	he doesn't have to do it he hasn't got to do it	he mustn't do it
epistemic	(2)	he must be in		he can't be in
non-epistemic	(3)	he had to do it he'd got to do it	he didn't have to do it he hadn't got to do it	
epistemic	(4)	he must have been in		he couldn't have been in he can't have been in
	(5)	he'll have to do it	he won't have to do it	

The forms in the **negative modal** column have the meaning 'he is not compelled to do it (but he can if he likes)', while the forms in the negative main verb column have the meaning 'he is compelled not to do it'. The **epistemic** uses (rows 2 and 4) are those where inferences are being drawn: 'it is certain that he is in (because I can hear his radio)', etc. It can be seen that in Standard English in the south of England (the variety most often described in grammar books) only *must* appears in (c) and only *have to* or *have got to* in (b). It will also be seen that 3(c) and 5(c) are blank, because there is no way of saying 'he must not do it' in the past or future: one has to use constructions such as 'he wasn't allowed to do it' or 'he won't be allowed to do it'. In the north of England, however, these gaps are filled. At 1(c), in these areas, it is possible to have *he hasn't to do it* (and, for some speakers, *he's not got to do it* or *he hasn't got to do it* – which are therefore ambiguous in a way they are not in the south of England) with the additional meaning *he mustn't do it*. Similarly, with the past, 3(c), educated northern English can have *he hadn't to do it*, as well as *he didn't have to do it* and *he hadn't got to do it* or *he'd not got to do it*, which are again ambiguous. And for the future, 5(c), northern speakers have *he'll not have to do it* or *he won't have to do it* (which are ambiguous) and even *he'll haven't to do it*.

At 2(c) and 4(c) the usual northern forms are *he mustn't be in* and *he mustn't have been in*. And for many younger speakers in both the north and the south, probably as the result of North American influence, *have to* and *have got to* have also acquired epistemic use, particularly in positive, present tense usage. Thus *he must be the greatest player* in the world can now also be *he's got to be the greatest player in the world* or *he has to be the greatest player in the world*.

5 **It is possible to divide English verbs into two main classes according (among other criteria) to whether or not they employ** *auxiliary do* **in negatives and interrogatives:**

He walked	*He didn't walk*	*Did he walk?*
He laughed	*She didn't laugh*	*Did she laugh?*
She can leave	*She can't leave*	*Can she leave?*
He will go	*He won't go*	*Will he go?*

Verbs of the second type (without *do*) come into the category of modals and auxiliaries.

(a) The verbs *ought to* and *used to* are often described in English grammars as coming into this second category, and indeed are employed in this way by some older speakers:

He ought not to go	*Ought he to go?*
They used not to go	*Used they to go?*

With younger speakers, however – and this is particularly true of the interrogative form, especially with *used to* – these verbs are being reclassified in the first category:

He didn't ought to go	*Did he ought to go?*
They didn't use to go	*Did they use to go?*

(b) There is considerable regional and age-related variation concerning the verb *to have*. This variation concerns the extent to which *have* is treated as an auxiliary verb or as a **full** verb in different varieties of English.

In examining this variation, it is necessary to distinguish between **stative** meanings of the verb *to have* and **dynamic** meanings. With stative meanings, we are dealing with some kind of stable quality or state of affairs, where *to have* means something like 'to be in possession of'. With dynamic meanings, we are dealing with some kind of activity or temporary state of affairs, where the verb means something like 'to consume', 'to take', etc. Thus, *I have some coffee in the cupboard* involves stative meaning, whereas *I have coffee with my breakfast* is dynamic.

In English English, until relatively recently, the verb *to have* required **do-support** – that is, it was treated like a full verb – in the case of dynamic meanings only. Thus:

Does she have coffee with breakfast?	*No, she doesn't*
They didn't have a good time last night	

With stative meanings, on the other hand, it was treated as an auxiliary and did not require *do*-support. Thus:

Have they any money?	*No, they haven't*
They hadn't any coffee in the cupboard	

In American English, on the other hand, *do*-support is required in both cases, so the verb *to have* is treated as a main verb regardless of whether it has dynamic or stative meanings. Thus:

> *Does she have coffee with breakfast?*   *No, she doesn't*
> *They didn't have a good time last night*
> *Do they have any money?*   *No, they don't*
> *They didn't have any coffee in the cupboard*

In Scottish English and, to a certain extent in the north of England as well as in many parts of Ireland, we find the opposite situation – there is no distinction between dynamic and stative meanings, the verb *to have* being treated as an auxiliary in all cases. Thus, in addition to saying:

> *Have they any money?*   *No, they haven't*
> *They hadn't any coffee in the cupboard*

in Scottish English one can also say:

> *Has she coffee with her breakfast?*   *No, she hasn't*
> *They hadn't a good time last night*

though this is probably used more rarely by younger Scottish people than it is by people of their grandparents' generation.

This difference in the status of *have* is also demonstrated by different possibilities of phonological contraction (only auxiliary *have* can be contracted). Thus:

> US English   *I have no money*   *I had a good time*
> English English   *I've no money*   *I had a good time*
> Scottish English   *I've no money*   *I'd a good time*

In both American and British English, it is also very usual with stative meanings in more informal styles to use the *have got* construction, for example:

> *Have they got any money?*   *No, they haven't*
> *They hadn't got any coffee in the cupboard*

There is also the further complication that the American-style lack of grammatical distinction between stative and dynamic meanings has had an influence on the English of England, particularly among younger southern speakers. This means that in southern England English we now have the possibility, with stative meanings, of using three different types of construction:

> *Have you got any money?*   (informal)
> *Have you any money?*   (formal, older)
> *Do you have any money?*   (newer)

6   **It is well known that certain *verb–particle* constructions in English have alternative forms as follows:**

(a) *He turned out the light*   *Put on your coat!*   *She took off her shoes*

(b) *He turned the light out*   *Put your coat on!*   *She took her shoes off*

There is, however, regional variation with respect to this usage in Britain. All speakers will accept both (a) and (b) as normal English, but speakers in the south of England are more likely to employ the (b) forms in their own speech, whereas Scottish speakers very frequently use forms of type (a).

7   *Like*

Like is becoming increasingly frequent in the speech of younger British and Irish people, regardless of whether they speak standard or non-standard dialects. *Like* fulfils several functions: it can function as a **pause filler**, as in

> *Are you, like, coming to the cinema tonight?*

as well as a **focus marker**, serving to draw attention to a following piece of information:

> *It was like the funniest film I've ever seen.*

It can also function, with the verb *be*, as a means of directly reporting speech (equivalent to *said*, etc.) or a person's (unverbalized) emotional status, as in

> *They were like, 'I hate this place,' but she's like, just shut up both of you.*

This last function of *like* is termed **quotative (*be*) *like*** (see Tagliamonte and Hudson 1999; Dailey-O'Cain 2000), and it is thought to have been imported fairly recently into British English from North America. Note that the Leicester speaker on the CD uses *like* very frequently for all three functions (see Chapter 5, p. 91).

Lexical features

We shall be dealing further with variation in vocabulary in individual sections. It is worth noting here, however, that some features, such as the lack of distinction between *teach* and *learn*, and between *borrow* and *lend*, are found in nearly all non-standard dialects:

> *They don't learn you nothing at school* (= *They don't teach you anything at school*)
>
> *Can I lend your bike?* (= *Can I borrow your bike?*)

Features of colloquial style

At some points it is difficult to distinguish between features of colloquial style and those of non-standard dialect. The following are a few of these.

(a) *us* can function as the first person singular object pronoun:

Give us a kiss!

(b) **pronoun apposition** – a personal pronoun immediately following its antecedent noun:

My dad he told me not to

(c) **indefinite *this*** – *this* can function as an indefinite article, particularly in narratives:

There's this house, see, and there's this man with a gun

Non-standard grammatical forms

In this book we cannot provide a comprehensive list of all the grammatical differences to be found between non-standard British dialects and Standard English; readers are recommended to look at Milroy and Milroy (1993) for further information on the topic. We can, however, describe some of the forms most common in varieties, and point out the types of differences to be looked for in each area, and will do so, briefly, in this chapter. Further examples, together with instances of lexical variation, will be cited in the individual sections of Chapter 5.

Multiple negation

There are a number of grammatical forms which differ from those in Standard English and which can be found in most parts of the British Isles. This is because, in these cases, it is in fact the standard dialect which has diverged from the other varieties, not the other way round.

A good example of this is the grammatical construction well known throughout the English-speaking world as 'the double negative'. If we take a sentence in Standard English such as

I had some dinner

we can note that there are two different ways of making this sentence negative. We can either negate the verb:

I didn't have any dinner

or we can negate the word *some*, by changing it to *no*:

I had no dinner

These sentences do have different stylistic connotations, the latter being more formal, but they mean approximately the same thing.

The main point is that in Standard English one can perform one or other of these operations, but not both. In most other English dialects, however, one can do both these things at once. The result is **multiple negation**:

> *I didn't have no dinner*

(Linguists prefer the terms multiple negation or **negative concord** to the more common term 'double negative', since the construction is not limited to two negatives. It is possible to have three or more, as in *she couldn't get none nowhere*).

It is safe to say that constructions of the type *I didn't have no dinner* are employed by the majority of English speakers, both in the British Isles and worldwide. At one time this construction was found in the standard dialect, too, and it has parallels in many other languages (such as the *ne . . . pas* construction in French). It is, however, considered to be 'wrong' by many people in the English-speaking world. This is largely because it is, like most non-standard grammatical forms, most typical of working-class speech, and for that reason tends to have low prestige. People who believe it to be 'wrong', 'ugly', 'clumsy' or 'illogical' are, we can say, probably making what is ultimately a social rather than linguistic judgement. It would be interesting to know whether these people would still look on multiple negation so disapprovingly if it were pointed out to them that both Chaucer and Shakespeare used these constructions in their writing.

There is, in addition, considerable regional variation in the type of constructions in which multiple negation is permitted. The following sorts of construction occur in some non-standard dialects but not in others:

> *We haven't got only one* (= Standard English *We've only got one*)
> *He went out without no shoes on*

Other aspects of negation in non-standard dialects

Unlike multiple negation, the form *ain't* is not found throughout Britain, but it is nevertheless extremely common. It is variously pronounced /eɪnt/, /ɛnt/, or /ɪnt/, and has two main functions. First, it corresponds to the negative forms of the present tense of *be* in Standard English, i.e. *aren't*, *isn't*, and *am not*:

> *I ain't coming*   *He/she/it ain't there*   *You/we/they ain't going*

Secondly, it functions as the negative present tense of auxiliary *have*, corresponding to Standard English *haven't* and *hasn't*:

> *I ain't done it*   *He ain't got one*

Note, however, that it does not usually function as the negative present form of the full verb *have*:

> **I ain't a clue* (= *I haven't a clue*)

(The asterisk indicates an unacceptable construction.)

The form *aren't* also occurs more widely in non-standard dialects than in Standard English. In Standard English, of course, it occurs as the negation of *are*, as in *we aren't, you aren't, they aren't*. It also occurs in the first person singular with the interrogative *aren't I?* But in some non-standard dialects the form *I aren't*, equivalent to Standard English *I'm not*, also occurs, while *I amn't* occurs in parts of the West Midlands and in Scotland.

Past tense of irregular verbs

Regular verbs in English have identical forms for the past tense and for the past participle, as used in the formation of perfect verb forms:

Present	*Past*	*Present perfect*
I work	*I worked*	*I have worked*
I love	*I loved*	*I have loved*

Many **irregular** verbs, on the other hand, have in Standard English distinct forms for the past tense and past participle:

Present	*Past*	*Present perfect*
I see	*I saw*	*I have seen*
I go	*I went*	*I have gone*
I come	*I came*	*I have come*
I write	*I wrote*	*I have written*

In many non-standard dialects, however, there is a strong tendency to bring the irregular verbs into line with the regular ones, the distinction being signalled only by the presence or absence of *have*. There is considerable regional variation here, but in some cases we find the original past participle used also as the past tense form:

Present	*Past*	*Present perfect*
I see	*I seen*	*I have seen*
I go	*I went*	*I have went*
I come	*I come*	*I have come*
I write	*I wrote*	*I have wrote*

(In the case of *come*, as with *hit*, *put*, *cut*, etc. in Standard English, all three forms are identical.)

In other cases, **levelling** has taken place in the other direction:

Present	**Past**	**Present perfect**
I see	*I saw*	*I have saw*
I go	*I went*	*I have went*

And in others, the present tense form may be generalized:

Present	**Past**	**Present perfect**
I see	*I see*	*I have seen*
I give	*I give*	*I have given*

We can also note common forms such as:

Present	**Past**	**Present perfect**
I write	*I writ* /ɪɪt/	*I have writ*

and the continuation of the historical tendency (known as **analogical levelling**) to make irregular verbs regular:

Present	**Past**	**Present perfect**
I draw	*I drawed*	*I have drawed*

The verb *do* is also involved in social dialect variation of this type, and in a rather interesting way. As is well known to learners of English as a foreign language, *do* has two functions. It can act as a full verb, as in:

> *He's doing maths at school*   *I did lots of work*

and it can also act as an auxiliary verb, and is used as such in interrogation, negation, emphasis, and 'code' (Palmer 1988):

> *Did you go?*   *You went, did you?*   *We didn't go*
> *I did like it*   *We went and so did they*

In Standard English, the forms of the full verb and of the auxiliary are identical:

> *He does maths, does he?*   *You did lots of work, didn't you?*

In most non-standard dialects, however, the full verb and the auxiliary are distinguished in the past tense, as the full verb has been subjected to the levelling process described above, while the auxiliary has not. That is, the past tense form of the full verb is *done*, and that of the auxiliary *did*:

> *You done lots of work, didn't you?*   *I done it last night*
> **A:** *Did you?* **B:** *Yes, I did*

These non-standard dialects therefore have a grammatical distinction that is not found in the standard dialect. This example is one of many that demonstrate that non-standard dialects are not grammatically deficient or incomplete relative to Standard English, as many people think: the grammars of non-standard varieties are just different from that of Standard English, and are equally as complex.

'Never' as past tense negative

In non-standard dialects in most parts of the British Isles the word *never*, in contrast to Standard English, can refer to a single occasion, and functions in the same way as the form *didn't*. Thus *I never done it* means *I did not do it* with reference to a single, particular occasion (for example, if a child is trying to deny having broken a window by kicking a football through it). Forms of this type are particularly common in the speech of children, but are well attested in adult speech too:

> *I never went to the shops today after all*   **A:** *You done it!*   **B:** *I never!*

Present tense verb forms

The present tense form of the verb in Standard English is somewhat anomalous with regard to other dialects of the language in that the third person singular form is distinguished from the other forms by the presence of -*s*:

> *I want*
> *you want*
> *we want*   but   *he ~ she ~ it wants*
> *they want*

In a number of non-standard dialects, this anomaly is not found. In East Anglia, as in some American and Caribbean varieties, this verb paradigm is completely regular as a result of the absence of the third singular -*s*. In these dialects, forms such as the following are usual:

> *She like him*   *It go very fast*   *He want it*   *He don't like it*

The individual form *don't*, in fact, is very common indeed throughout the English-speaking world in the third person singular.

In other parts of Britain, including parts of the north of England and especially the south-west and South Wales, the regularity is of the opposite kind, with -*s* occurring with all persons of the verb:

> *I likes it*   *We goes home*   *You throws it*

In parts of the west of England this leads to the complete distinction of the full verb *do* and auxiliary *do*:

	Present	*Past*	*Past participle*
Full verb:	*dos* /duːz/	*done*	*done*
Auxiliary:	*do*	*did*	–

Thus:

> *He dos it every day, do he?*   *He done it last night, did he?*

In other dialects, including many in Scotland and Northern Ireland, the forms with *-s* in the first and second persons and in the third person plural are a sign of the **historic present**, where the present tense is used to make the narration of past events more vivid:

> *I go home every day at four o'clock*

but

> *I goes down this street and I sees this man hiding behind a tree*

Relative pronouns

In Standard English, *who* is used as a **relative pronoun** referring to human nouns, *which* is used for non-human nouns, and *that* is used for nouns of both types. The relative pronoun is also frequently omitted in **restrictive relative clauses** where it refers to the object of a verb:

Human	*That was the man who did it*	*That was the man who I found*
	That was the man that did it	*That was the man that I found*
		That was the man I found
Non-human	*That was the brick which did it*	*That was the brick which I found*
	That was the brick that did it	*That was the brick that I found*
		That was the brick I found

These forms are also found in non-standard dialects, but a number of additional forms also occur, including omission (or **ellipsis**) of pronouns referring to the subject:

> *That was the man what done it*
> *That was the man which done it*
> *That was the man as done it*
> *That was the man at done it*
> *That was the man done it*

The form with *what* is particularly common. **Possessive relatives** (like *whose* in Standard English) may also differ from Standard English:

> *That's the man what his son done it* (= *That's the man whose son did it*)
> *This is the man that's son did it* (= *This is the man whose son did it*)

Personal pronouns

A number of interesting regional and social differences concerning the personal pronouns can be noted. These include the use in north-eastern England and in Scotland of *us* as a first person singular object pronoun, as in *He deliberately tripped us as I was walking down the corridor*. This phenomenon is also commonly found in the colloquial speech of many other parts of Britain, but in these places it is confined to a limited number of locutions, such as *Do us a favour* and *Give us a kiss*. Outside Scotland and north-eastern England, us (= me) is otherwise confined to indirect object status.

The **reflexive** pronouns in Standard English are formed by suffixing -*self* or -*selves* to

(a) the possessive pronoun:

my	*myself*
your	*yourself / yourselves*
our	*ourselves*

(b) the object pronoun:

him	*himself*
it	*itself*
them	*themselves*

The form *herself* could be regarded as being based on either the possessive or the object pronoun. Note also that because *they, their* and *them* are now very frequently used in the third person singular (as in the 'gender-neutral' *If they are a student on my course, tell them to get their essay in immediately*), the form *themself* can now be heard and read more and more often, as in *Every student should give themself a break from their studies*, or the American newspaper headline *Vandal should turn themself in*. Similarly, *ourself* is fairly common: its use might strike some modern readers or listeners as a sign of ignorance or inability to think logically, but in earlier forms of the language it was originally used interchangeably with *ourselves*, and can even be found in Dickens.

Many non-standard dialects have regularized the reflexive pronoun system so that, for instance, all forms are based on the possessives:

> *myself*
> *herself*

yourself
itself
hisself
ourselves
theirselves

In parts of northern England, notably Yorkshire, the suffix *-sen* is used where Standard English has *-self*, so that the equivalent of himself is *hissen* /ɪˈsɛn/.

Comparatives and superlatives

Standard English permits comparison through either the addition of *more*:

She's more beautiful than you

or through the addition of *-er*:

He's nicer

Many non-standard dialects permit both **comparative** forms simultaneously:

She's more rougher than he is

The same is also true with **superlatives**. Since Shakespeare wrote *The most unkindest cut of all* this form has been lost in Standard English, but it survives in many other dialects:

He's the most roughest bloke I've ever met

In many non-standard dialects, the comparative and superlative suffixes can be attached to adjectives which do not allow this in Standard English:

You ought to be carefuller in future
She's the beautifullest woman I know

Demonstratives

Corresponding to the Standard English system of

this   *these*
that   *those*

a number of social and regional variants occur. Most commonly, Standard English *those* corresponds to *them* in non-standard dialects, but particularly in Scottish dialects *they* (sometimes spelled *thae*) can also be heard.

Look at them animals!
Look at they animals!

The forms *yon* and *thon* are also used in Scotland (see under Traditional dialects (e) on p. 34).

Adverbs

In Standard English, there are many pairs of formally related adjectives and adverbs:

> *He was a slow runner*   *He ran slowly*
> *She was a very clever speaker*   *She spoke very cleverly*

In most non-standard dialects, these forms are not distinct:

> *He ran slow*   *She spoke very clever*   *They done it very nice*
>   cf. *He'll do it very good*

In the case of some adverbs, forms without -*ly* are also found in colloquial Standard English:

> *Come quick!*

although some speakers might not accept this as Standard English.

Unmarked plurality

A very widespread feature indeed in many non-standard dialects involves nouns of measurement following numerals not being marked for plurality:

> *a hundred pound*   *thirteen mile*   *five foot*

The use of *foot* in plural contexts like those above is not unheard of in colloquial Standard English.

Prepositions of place

Prepositions exhibit a large degree of variation in their usage in British dialects. This is particularly true of prepositions of place, and we can do no more here than cite a very few examples of cases where non-standard dialects can differ from Standard English:

> *He went up the park* (= *He went to the park*)
> *We walked down the shops* (= *We walked to the shops*)
> *I got off of the bus* (= *I got off the bus*)
> *It was at London* (= *It was in London*)

Note that *at* was formerly frequently used in Standard English when describing locations in large towns or cities, as in for example *My parents learned to dance at Oxford* (= *in Oxford* in contemporary Standard English).

In modern Standard English, the use of *at* with proper names of this sort often implies more specific meanings: *at Oxford* in the above example would probably be understood to mean *at the University of Oxford* by most British people today. In other cases, such as *You need to change at Oxford* or *He was arrested on his arrival at Manchester*, a particular location within the town or city is meant (in these examples, Oxford's railway or bus station and Manchester Airport, respectively).

Traditional dialects

In most of this book, we deal chiefly with those accents and dialects of English in the British Isles which foreign visitors are most likely to come into contact with. In this section, however, we deal briefly with certain grammatical features associated in particular with what are often referred to as 'traditional dialects'.

Traditional dialects are those conservative dialects of English which are, for the most part, spoken in relatively isolated rural areas by certain older speakers and which differ considerably from Standard English, and indeed from one another. Traditional dialects are what most British people think of when they hear the term 'dialect' used in a non-technical way. They correspond to those varieties which are known as *patois* in the French-speaking world and *Mundart* in German-speaking areas.

Grammatical features which are typical of certain traditional dialects include the following:

(a) In most Scottish dialects, negation is not formed with *not*, but with *no* or with its more typically Scottish forms *nae* /ne/ or *na* /na/. Thus we find forms in Scottish English such as:

He's no coming	*I've nae got it*
I cannae go	*We do na have one*

(b) In large areas of the north of England, including urban areas of Yorkshire, as well as in many areas of the rural south-west of England, the older distinction still survives between the informal singular second person pronouns *thou*, *thee*, *thine* and formal and/or plural *you* ~ *yours*. In the north of England, the usual subject and object form of this pronoun is *tha*, while in the south-west it tends to be *thee*. The system operates very much as in modern French, with friends and family being referred to as *tha* and people who one does not know so well being called *you*. It is also sometimes the case that distinct verb forms associated with second person singular still survive; for example, *tha cast* 'you can'.

(c) In large areas of the south-west of England, including Devon and Somerset, a system of personal pronouns exists in which the form of the pronoun is not, for the most part, determined by subject versus object function, but by weak or strong **stress** position. For example:

strong	weak
you	ee
he	er (subject), 'n (object)
she	er
we	us
they	'm

Thus: *You wouldn't do that, would ee?*
He wouldn't do that, would er?
No, give 'n to he
She wouldn't do that, would er?
No, give 'n to she
We wouldn't do that, would us?
No, give 'n to we
They wouldn't do that, would 'm?
No, give 'm to they

(d) In many traditional dialects of the south-west of England, the gender system operates in a manner unlike that existing in Standard English, in that **mass** nouns such as *water* and *bread* are usually referred to as *it*, while **count** nouns such as *hammer* and *tree* are referred to as *he, er,* or *'n*. Thus one would say:

Pass me the bread. It's on the table
but *Pass me the loaf. He's on the table*

(e) In areas of the north of England and in Scotland, a three-way distinction in the system of demonstratives, rather than the two-way system associated with Standard English, can be found (see for example McRae 2000).

Singular	Plural (northern England)	Plural (Scotland)
this	these	thir
that	them	they ~ thae
yon	yon	yon ~ thon

Some traditional dialects in northern Scotland do not use *thir* and *they ~ thae* in plural contexts, but instead use the singular form, as in

This plates is too small
My nephew drew that pictures

(f) Forms of the verb *to be*, particularly those in the present tense, show much greater variation in traditional dialects than in more modern forms of speech. For example, in the north-east of England, *is* is generalized to all persons – for example, *I is*. In parts of the West Midlands, *am* may be generalized to all persons, as in *you am*, while in areas of south-western England, *be* may be generalized to all persons of the verb – that is, *you be, he be, they be*, etc.

(g) In Aberdeen, as in north-eastern Scotland generally, **tags** such as *is(n't) it, do(n't) they*, and so forth, have a tendency to agree in **polarity** (positive vs. negative) with the statement they attach to. So while in Standard English the usual way to elicit the listener's agreement with a positive statement is to add a negative tag, as in

 It's a fine day, isn't it?

speakers from north-eastern Scotland are very frequently heard to use a **same-polarity tag**, as in

 It's a fine day, is it?

While the positive tag *is it?* may of course be used in this context in Standard English, its use in that dialect serves to indicate either that the speaker does not know whether it is in fact a fine day (for instance, while discussing the weather with an Australian relative by telephone), or is used when he/she is (often sarcastically or aggressively) contradicting another's assertion that it is a fine day when the evidence is to the contrary.

3 Received pronunciation

In this chapter we begin by presenting a framework for the description of the sounds of English. We then outline the principal ways in which RP varies, before going on to look in detail at the sounds of RP. We do not discuss stress, rhythm, or intonation in any detail in connection with this accent, or with the others described in later chapters, as they are beyond the scope of this book (see Wells 1982 and Cruttenden 2001 for information on these topics).

A framework for description

Consonants and vowels

We must begin by making a distinction between **consonants** and **vowels**. Because our interest is in pronunciation, this distinction is based on the spoken, not the written language: what we will refer to as vowels are therefore *not* the letters *a*, *e*, *i*, *o*, and *u*. Letters, it must be remembered, is the name we give to marks on paper or patterns of light and dark on computer screens. Speech sounds – which exist in the domain of acoustics and hearing, and are produced by various movements of the speech organs – are therefore clearly very different things from the visual symbols we use to represent them, and we should be careful not to talk about symbols and sounds as though they were at all similar.

The first criterion for assigning sounds to the vowel category is that their production does not involve **closure**, such that the airflow from the lungs to the outside air is cut off (as in the initial and final sounds of the words *pat* and *bag*), or narrowing of the **vocal tract** to the extent that audible friction is created (as in the initial and final sounds of *fizz* and *sash*).

The second criterion is that they should typically occur in the middle of a **syllable**, rather than at its margins. The middle portion of a syllable is called its **nucleus**. All other sounds, including those that meet the first criterion but not the second (the first sounds of the words *run*, *lend*, *young*, *wing*) are, not surprisingly, categorized as consonants.

Describing consonants

Consonants are described in terms of the presence or absence of **voicing** (vibration of the **vocal folds**), **place of articulation**, and **manner of articulation**. Thus the initial sound in the word *vat* is said to be a voiced labiodental fricative: the vocal folds (or **cords**) vibrate, and the sound is created by friction of the air as it passes through a narrow gap between lip (*labio-*) and teeth (*dental*). By contrast, the initial sound in the word *fat* is a voiceless labiodental fricative, the difference between it and the first sound in *vat* being that in the first sound of *fat* there is no vibration of the vocal folds. And the initial sound of *sat* is termed a voiceless alveolar fricative. In this sound the friction is created as air rushes through the narrow gap between the tongue and the **alveolar ridge**.

We can check whether or not a sound is voiced by putting our fingers in our ears while saying the sound – the vibrations created by the vocal folds for voiced sounds are much more readily heard this way. Alternatively, we can put thumb and forefinger on either side of the cartilage at the front of the **larynx** (that is, the Adam's apple). If any voicing is present in the sound, we can feel vibration through our fingertips. If we want to check the place of articulation of a consonant, we can often get a sense of where in the mouth the sound is being produced by uttering the sound on the in-breath (i.e. while breathing in instead of out). The point at which the vocal tract is narrowest – most constricted – will feel somewhat colder than other parts of the mouth, because the air rushing inwards towards the lungs has to travel faster to squeeze through the narrow gap.

All of the consonants referred to in this book are to be found in the current chart of the International Phonetic Alphabet (IPA) symbols on p. ix, which shows for each of them their place and manner of articulation, and whether or not they are voiced.

Describing vowels

Vowels are customarily described in terms of: (a) the part of the tongue which is raised towards the roof of the mouth in producing it, and how far it is raised; and (b) how spread or rounded the lips are. Much of this information can be captured through the use of **cardinal vowel** charts, which we will be using throughout the remainder of the book. These charts are based on the Cardinal Vowel system devised by Daniel Jones early in the twentieth century. This system of sixteen vowel sounds relates to the sounds produced when the highest part of the tongue (relative to the floor) is in eight different positions – there are four at the front of the mouth, and four at the back – with the lips either **rounded** or **unrounded**.

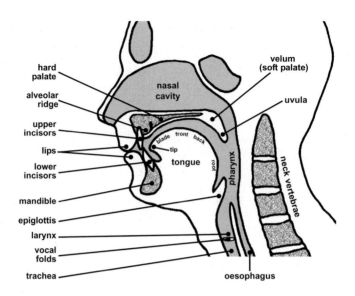

Figure 3.1
Schematized mid-sagittal section of the human head, showing the organs of speech

The cardinal vowel **quadrilateral** can also be found on the IPA chart on p. ix. It shows the position of the sixteen cardinal vowels, as well as a number of **central** vowels. The chart is a schematic representation of the mouth, with **close** referring to a position of the tongue as close to the **hard palate** as possible without friction occurring, and with **open** referring to a position of the tongue at the bottom of the mouth, with a marked degree of jaw opening. A feeling can be developed for the relationship between symbols at various positions in the vowel chart and the sounds they represent by listening to speakers reading the word list (p. xi) on the CD, while identifying the position of the vowels on the relevant vowel chart.

Phonemes and allophones

The initial sounds of the words *fan* and *van* are clearly different. As we saw above, the first is voiceless and the second voiced. But not only are the two sounds different from each other, they also make a difference of meaning. A *fan* is not the same thing as a *van*.

In RP (but not in every accent of English), the initial sound of the word *leaf* is not the same as the final sound of the word *feel*. The first is said to be **clear**, and the second (which involves the back of the tongue being drawn towards the **velum** or soft palate) is referred to as **dark**. In this case, however, the difference does *not* affect meaning. If we began the word *leaf* with a dark *l* rather than a clear *l*, the word would not change in meaning. Whether we used a dark *l* or a clear *l*, we would be understood to be referring to a leaf.

All four consonants referred to in the previous two paragraphs can be represented by phonetic symbols. In order to represent sounds phonetically, we place the symbols between square brackets. We have [f] and [v], [l] (clear) and [ɫ] (dark). Dark [ɫ] is often also represented by [lˠ] – the small superscripted symbol meaning 'velarized' – but the same sound is meant.

Although there are four physically different sounds, two of them – [l] and [ɫ] – are not **contrastive**: they do not have the capacity to change words' meanings in English. For this reason they may be considered as different realizations of a single linguistic unit. Such a unit is referred to as a **phoneme**, and its different realizations as **allophones**.

Phonemes are represented between slant brackets. Thus we can say that the phoneme /l/ has two allophones, [l] and [ɫ]. This allows us to give two possible transcriptions of, for instance, the word *feel*. A **phonemic** transcription would be /fiːl/, while a more detailed, *phonetic* transcription would be [fiːɫ]. The usefulness of the distinction between phonemes and allophones will become apparent below.

Variability in RP

Even though we speak of RP as a single accent, there is nevertheless significant variability within it. In this section we will begin by identifying the forms that variability takes and then go on to discuss the factors that account for variability.

Forms of variability

There are three main forms of variability in RP: **systemic**, **realizational**, and **lexical**. We speak of systemic or **inventory** variability when different speakers have different sets (or 'systems') of phonemes. In RP this now applies only to vowel phonemes. Some older speakers of RP have one more vowel phoneme than others. Such speakers distinguish between pairs of words like *paw* and *pore*, pronouncing them /pɔː/ and /pɔə/ respectively. Most other RP speakers do not have the vowel /ɔə/, and pronounce both words /pɔː/.

Realizational variability refers to the way in which a single phoneme may have different phonetic realizations. For example, all RP speakers have a phoneme /əʊ/ (as in *boat*), which contrasts with /eɪ/ (*bait*), /aʊ/ (*bout*), and /aɪ/ (*bite*). They do not all pronounce it in the same way, however. Older speakers may pronounce the vowel as [oʊ], with a back first element, although this is now very old-fashioned in RP. The vowel phoneme of younger speakers, however, starts from a more central point, giving [bəʊt].

In the context of pronunciation, lexical variability refers to the use of different series of phonemes for the same word. We have already noted one example in Chapter 1, the pronunciation of *economic* as /iːkəˈnɒmɪk/ or /ɛkəˈnɒmɪk/, both of which are found amongst RP speakers. Another example is the different pronunciation of the word *off*, which may be /ɒf/ (rhyming with *cough*, and by far the most usual pronunciation) or the now archaic /ɔːf/ (rhyming with *wharf*, and usually associated with older, upper-class speakers).

All of the variability referred to above relates to individual words and to differences of pronunciation between people. In continuous speech there is further variability, some of which depends on the speed and formality of speech as much as it does on differences between people. This variability includes a number of processes: H-dropping (e.g. /ˈstɒp ɪm/ for *stop him*); R-insertion (e.g. /vəˈnɪləɹ aɪsˈkriːm/ for *vanilla ice-cream*); elision, as in the example in Chapter 1 of /ˈspɛk səʊ/ for *expect so*; and assimilation, as in our earlier example /ðap pleɪt/ *that plate*. We describe conditions for H-dropping and R-insertion in the sections on the /h/ and /ɹ/ phonemes (pp. 44, 46).

Factors accounting for variability

There are several factors which help to account for variability within RP. The first of these is the age of the speaker. Like any living accent, RP is constantly changing, and so there will be differences between the pronunciation of younger and older speakers. As we noted above, older speakers may have one more vowel phoneme in their system than do most other speakers of the accent. Younger speakers typically use more glottal stops (see pp. 42–3) than their elders, and use monophthongs where diphthongs have been traditional (see pp. 4, 51–3).

A second factor is social class. Members of the upper classes have features which distinguish them from the majority of RP speakers. In identifying this social stratum, Wells (1982) refers to dowager duchesses, certain army officers, Noël Coward-type sophisticates, and popular images of elderly Oxbridge dons and 'jolly-hockey-sticks' school-mistresses. Such speakers are likely to have, for example, a particularly open final vowel in words like *university*, something close to cardinal vowel 3, [ɛ]. Such pronunciations appear to be receding, however, and it has even been claimed that members of the British royal family, including the Queen, no longer use 'upper-class' RP features of this sort.

A third factor is the age at which a person began to acquire an RP accent. Those who acquire it after childhood are likely to avoid normal features of faster RP speech, such as the dropping of unaccented /h/ in pronouns.

Other personal factors include the particular school attended; the speaker's profession or role; personality (a fastidious person may avoid something they consider vulgar, such as use of glottal stops for /t/ in certain environments); attitudes to language and to other speakers of RP; the frequency with which a speaker uses a word (less frequently used words being less likely to participate in a general change of pronunciation – for example, for some speakers at least, *heir* is less likely to be monophthongized than *air*); and even what a person has been told, perhaps by a teacher, is the 'correct' pronunciation of a word.

Other authors have concentrated on some of these factors in identifying subvarieties of RP. For Gimson (1988) there were three main types: *conservative RP*, spoken by the older generation and certain professional and social groups; *general RP*, the least marked variety; and *advanced RP*, spoken by younger members of exclusive social groups. Cruttenden's (2001) revision of Gimson's book uses the labels *General*, *Refined* and *Regional RP*. Cruttenden's *Refined RP* is equivalent to Gimson's *conservative RP*, while his apparently contradictory *Regional RP* refers to 'the type of speech which is basically RP except for the presence of a few regional characteristics which go unnoticed even by other speakers of RP' (Cruttenden 2001: 80). These, he argues, include features like the use of /l/-**vocalization**, whereby a word-final /l/ is realized as a vowel such as [ʊ] to give, for example, [bɔʊ] for *ball*, although in modern RP it would be difficult to maintain that /l/-vocalization can any longer be described as a regional feature.

Wells (1982) also proposes three significant varieties: *u-RP* (upper-crust RP), spoken by the group identified as upper class above; *mainstream RP*, equivalent to Gimson's *general RP*; and *adoptive RP*, spoken by those who acquire the accent after childhood. In the following section, for each sound we begin by describing mainstream RP and then identify and comment on any significant variants.

The individual sounds of RP

Consonants

In this section, we describe the consonants in sets based on their manner of articulation.

Plosives

Plosives involve three stages: first, a closure in some part of the vocal tract, then the compression of air as it builds up behind the obstruction, and finally the release of that compressed air in the form of an explosion as the blockage is removed (hence the name 'plosive'). There are six plosive phonemes in RP:

	bilabial	alveolar	velar
voiceless	/p/	/t/	/k/
voiced	/b/	/d/	/g/

The voiceless plosives /p, t, k/ are usually marked by **aspiration**, an interval of voicelessness between the plosive release and the onset of the following sound. We transcribe these aspirated plosives phonetically as [pʰ, tʰ, kʰ]. There is no aspiration, however, when the plosive follows /s/ initially in a syllable, as in /spɪn/ *spin*. Aspiration may also be absent from these plosives at the end of a word, particularly in informal speech. According to Wells (1982), stressed word-initial /p, t, k/ often have surprisingly little aspiration in the speech of upper-class speakers.

The duration of vowels (particularly long vowels) before /p, t, k/ is shorter than when they occur before /b, d, g/. Thus, for example, the vowel /iː/ in *bead* is of somewhat greater duration than when it occurs in *beat*.

The place of articulation of the alveolar plosives /t, d/ is strongly influenced by that of a following consonant. Before /θ/ (in *eighth*, for example) /t/ will be a dental [t̪]; before /ɹ/ (in *drugs*, for example) /d/ will be a post-alveolar [d̠].

The place of articulation of the velar plosives /k, g/ depends on the quality of the accompanying vowel. With /iː/, as in *leak*, the /k/ may be realized as a palatal [c]; with /ɑː/, as in *lark*, the closure will be significantly further back.

Where two plosives occur together, either within a word or on either side of a word boundary (as in *act* or *bad boy*), the first plosive is not released. When a plosive occurs before a nasal consonant (as in *could not*), the release is nasal: that is, the oral release is achieved by lowering the velum to allow the pressurized air to escape through the nasal cavity, rather than out of the mouth. When a plosive occurs before /l/ (e.g. *bottle* /bɒtl̩/), the release is lateral, i.e. the air escapes as a result of the raising of one or both sides of the tongue.

The glottal stop [ʔ] is a form of plosive in which the closure is made by bringing the vocal folds together, as when holding one's breath (the **glottis** is not a speech organ as such, but is the space between the vocal folds). Some readers may be surprised to learn that the glottal stop has long been a feature of RP, though it does not have phonemic status and goes largely unnoticed in the accent. It is used by some speakers to reinforce /p, t, k, tʃ/ in a range of syllable-final environments. In such cases the glottal stop precedes the consonant, as in e.g. *six* [sɪʔks], this process being referred to as **glottalization**. The glottal stop may also mark a syllable boundary when the following syllable begins with a vowel, or stand in place of a **linking** or **intrusive** /ɹ/ (see below).

The glottal stop is frequently used as a realization of word- or morpheme-final /p, t, k/ when followed by a consonant. Thus ['skɒʔlənd] for *Scotland*, ['gaʔwɪk] for *Gatwick*, [geʔ'daʊn] for *get down*. The realization of /p/ and /k/ as [ʔ] is usually restricted to cases when the following consonant has the same place of articulation as that being realized as [ʔ], as in, for example, [baʔ 'gɑːdn̩] for *back garden*. The realization of a consonant as a glottal stop is known as **glottalling**.

Recently there has been an extension of the use of the glottal stop as a realization of /t/ in RP. Younger speakers, upper- as well as middle-class, may be heard variably using a glottal stop in word-final position, either before a pause or even before a vowel, as in e.g. [ðaʔ] for *that* and [kwaɪʔ'ɔːfł] *quite awful*. It is at least possible that the increased use of the glottal stop in RP is in part attributable to the influence of popular London speech (see Wells 1984; Tollfree 1999; Fabricius 2002). Careful speakers and speakers of adoptive RP will, however, tend to avoid glottalling.

Fricatives

Fricatives involve the speaker making a narrow gap between one articulator and another, causing friction as the air passing through it becomes turbulent. We can liken the turbulent airflow that produces fricative noise to the turbulence that occurs when smoothly flowing water is forced to flow through a narrow defile such as a canyon. There are nine fricative phonemes in RP.

	labio-dental	dental	alveolar	palato-alveolar	glottal
voiceless	/f/	/θ/	/s/	/ʃ/	/h/
voiced	/v/	/ð/	/z/	/ʒ/	

The voiced fricatives /v, ð, z, ʒ/ are in fact only partially voiced (or may be not voiced at all) when they occur word-finally, as in *of, breathe, dogs* and *rouge*. They may nonetheless still be distinct from their voiceless counterparts, however, by virtue of the greater duration of the vowel which precedes them, as we saw was the case for the plosives. For instance, the vowel /iː/ will have greater duration in *freeze* than in *fleece*.

The palato-alveolar fricative /ʒ/ occurs only word-medially (as in *measure*), except in French loan words such as *genre* and *prestige*, and in proper names from languages other than French, such as *Zhivago* or *Zsa Zsa*.

The glottal fricative /h/ only occurs in syllable-initial positions immediately preceding a vowel. The phonetic realization of /h/ depends on the quality of the vowel it precedes, since the sound is produced through the voiceless expulsion of air from the lungs with the mouth and tongue already in position for the following vowel. The sound of /h/ in *heat* is quite different from that in *heart*, for example. We could, therefore, think of /h/ as being a kind of voiceless vowel as well as a fricative, as Ladefoged and Maddieson (1996) have suggested.

As noted above, /h/ is usually dropped when it occurs in unstressed pronouns (*he, him, her, his*) and auxiliaries (*has, have, had*), thus ['stɒpɪm] for *stop him*. Careful speakers and speakers of adoptive RP are less likely to drop /h/, probably having been influenced by the stigma attached to more general H-dropping in other accents (see below).

Affricates

An affricate is a plosive with a sufficiently slow release for friction to occur during the release phase. In our analysis there are just two affricate phonemes: the palato-alveolar /tʃ/ and /dʒ/, which are voiceless and voiced respectively. Despite the fact that these sounds are composed of a distinct sequence of consonantal articulations and they are represented using two symbols rather than one, we analyse them as single units, since they function as such in English. No native English speaker would argue that the word *church* begins with the same sound as the word *table*, nor would he or she maintain that *church* ends with the same sound as does the word *fish*. Interestingly, the affricates also move as a unit when participating in the phenomenon known as **spoonerism**, whereby the speaker unintentionally swaps the initial sounds of two adjacent words. [bɜːtʃ tʃɛlz] is a plausible spoonerism for *church bells*, but [bʃɜːtʃ tɛlz] is not.

Nasals

Nasal consonants involve a closure somewhere within the mouth forward of the uvular place of articulation, but the velum is also lowered so that air can escape via the nasal cavity through the nostrils. There are three nasal phonemes in RP: bilabial /m/, alveolar /n/, and velar /ŋ/. They are normally all voiced, though there may be partial devoicing when they follow a voiceless consonant. All three nasals, but most commonly /n/, may be **syllabic**. Thus *button* may be /'bʌtn̩/.

The bilabial nasal /m/ and the alveolar nasal /n/ are normally realized as the labiodental [ɱ] where they precede /f/ or /v/. Thus, *comfort* will be ['kʰʌɱfət] and *invoice* ['ɪɱvɔɪs]. Before /θ/ and /ð/, as in *tenth* or *none there*, /n/ may be dental [n̪]; before /ɹ/, as in *unready*, it may be post-alveolar [n̠]. Some elderly upper-class RP speakers may retain /ɪn/ (rather than the usual /ɪŋ/) for the verbal ending *–ing*, thus /'fɪʃɪn/ for *fishing*. As the restricted age of those who display it implies, this feature seems to have declined markedly in frequency.

The velar nasal does not occur word-initially in native English words, though some speakers may make a point of attempting to pronounce proper names from Polynesian or African languages (like *Ngaio*, *Ngorongoro*, *Nkrumah* or *Nkomo*, all of which start with /ŋ/ in their source languages) using /ŋ/ in initial position.

Lateral /l/

Laterals involve the continuous escape of air around one or both sides of an obstruction formed by the tongue in the midline of the oral cavity. There is only one lateral phoneme in RP, which is normally voiced and which has three allophones. Two of these have been referred to above: clear [l], which is found before vowels (and /j/ in some very conservative pronunciations of words like *lewd* and *lure*); and dark [ɫ], which is found after a vowel, before a consonant, and syllabically e.g. ['bɒtɫ] for *bottle*. The third allophone is voiceless [l̥], which is most noticeable after aspirated /p/ and /k/, as in *plate* and *clap*.

Some RP speakers use a vowel in place of dark [ɫ] in certain environments, as in /'teɪbʊ/ *table* or /'bjuːtɪfʏ/ *beautiful*. This process, as we saw above, is known as /l/-vocalization. The actual quality of the vowel that substitutes for /l/ can be quite variable, but most are back and fairly close. The apparent increase in the vocalization of /l/ in RP may be coming about under the influence of popular London speech, where it is to be found more frequently and in a wider range of environments, as discussed in Chapter 5 (see also Przedlacka 2002). Since RP is far from alone among worldwide accents of English in its adoption of /l/-vocalization, however, we should treat this hypothesis with some caution (see Johnson and Britain 2005).

Post-alveolar approximant /ɹ/

The phoneme /ɹ/ occurs only before a vowel in RP. RP is thus a **non-rhotic** accent, and in this sense contrasts with **rhotic** accents such as those of Scotland, Ireland or North America, in which /ɹ/ may also occur after vowels within the syllable, as in /kɑːɹt/ *cart*. /ɹ/ in RP has a number of allophones. The most common is a voiced post-alveolar frictionless approximant [ɹ]. Following /d/ it is a fricative, [ɹ̝]. Following stressed /p, t, k/ it is typically devoiced, [ɹ̥]. **Intervocalically** (between vowels) when the first vowel is stressed, or following a dental fricative, /ɹ/ may be realized by the tip of the tongue tapping briefly against the alveolar ridge. This is the sound [ɾ], which is known as the alveolar tap, and in North America the alveolar flap. According to Wells (1982), this tapped [ɾ] is typical of some varieties of upper-class RP – it may be heard, for instance, in recordings of Noël Coward – though it is now rare in contemporary RP, even in emphatic pronunciations of relevant words.

When words which ended in /ɹ/ in earlier historical periods (as indicated by the spelling) are followed by a vowel-initial word, a **linking** /ɹ/ is normally introduced. Thus we have /fɑː/ *far*, but /ˈfɑːɹəˈweɪ/ *far away*.

Even when there is no historical /ɹ/, if a word ends with a non-high vowel (viz., /ə, ɔː, ɑː/) and precedes a word beginning with a vowel, again /ɹ/ may be inserted, thus /aɪ ˈsɔːɹɪt/ *I saw it*, /ˈmɑːɹəndˈpɑː/ *Ma and Pa*, or /ˈkanədəɹɔːˈmɛksɪkəʊ/ *Canada or Mexico*. Although in cases like these the /ɹ/ is referred to as **intrusive**, the phenomenon is very much a part of RP. Careful speakers and speakers of adoptive RP may, however, avoid it, possibly (as noted above) inserting a glottal stop between the words instead. Some speakers may even avoid the use of linking /ɹ/. Though still stigmatized by some, there is a very common tendency, as in many non-RP accents, for intrusive /ɹ/ to occur within words before a suffix, e.g. /ˈdɹɔːɹɪŋ/ for *drawing*, or recent coinings such as /ˌkafkəˈɹɛsk/ *Kafkaesque* or /daɪˌanəɹaɪˈzeɪʃn̩/ *Dianaization*.

Semi-vowels

There are two semi-vowel phonemes in English: the approximants /w/ and /j/. As noted earlier, though semi-vowels are vowel-like, they are treated as consonants because they function more like consonants, in the sense that they occupy syllable margins rather than acting as syllable nuclei.

The labial-velar semi-vowel /w/ is articulated with the tongue in a back close-mid position and with lip-rounding. It is normally voiced, but following /t/ (as in *twice*) or /k/ (as in *quick*) it is completely devoiced [w̥]. Consonants immediately preceding /w/ typically show anticipatory lip-rounding. Some RP speakers omit /w/ in some words that begin /kw/ for other speakers, thus /ˈkɔːtə/ *quarter*.

The palatal semi-vowel /j/ is articulated with the tongue in a front close-mid to close position. There may be lip-rounding in anticipation of a following rounded vowel. /j/ is normally voiced, but after accented /p, t, k, h/ (as in *pewter*, *tutor*, *cuter*, *huge*) there is complete devoicing, such that /j/ is realized as a palatal fricative [ç].

There is some lexical variation relating to the presence or absence of /j/ after /s/ and /l/ in such words as *suit* and *lute*, although these days pronunciations like /sjuːt/ are relatively rare. *Lute* and *loot* are now homophonous for most RP speakers.

There is a strong tendency for /j/ to **coalesce** with preceding alveolar plosives to form affricates, particularly in informal speech. By this process the sequence /tj/ (as in e.g. *tune*) becomes [tʃ] and /dj/ (as in *dune*) becomes [dʒ]. The pronunciation of *dune* would thus be indistinguishable from that of *June*. This coalescence – known as **yod-coalescence** – occurs when a word ending in /t/ or /d/ precedes *you* or *your*, e.g. [wɒtʃʊ'niːd] *what you need*, or [wʊdʒʊ] *would you.*

Within words, yod-coalescence is found most often where the second syllable involved is unstressed, e.g. *soldier* ['səʊldʒə]. Some careful speakers may try to avoid yod-coalescence in their speech, although many younger RP speakers consider this habit an affectation.

Vowels

Monophthongs

In our analysis of RP there are twelve **monophthongs** (sometimes called 'pure' vowels, because their quality does not change over the course of the vowel; compare **diphthongs**, below). Typical monophthong realizations are shown in Figure 3.2. We shall treat each of them in turn.

/iː/, as in *bee*
- The lips are spread.
- The vowel usually involves a **glide** (a transition in quality) from the position indicated for /ɪ/ in Figure 3.2 to that for /iː/. Pronunciation of this vowel without a glide is perceived as affected.
- There has been in recent decades a tendency for the final vowel in words like *city* and *very* to be rather closer and fronter than the 'traditional' /ɪ/, thus /'sɪti(ː)/ rather than the older /'sɪtɪ/. The plurals and possessive forms of such words, however, are more likely to contain /ɪ/, thus /'sɪtɪz/ for *cities* or *city's*, and older upper-class speakers may have a strikingly open final vowel in words like *city* ['sɪtɛ].

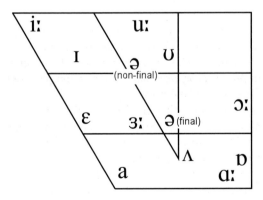

Figure 3.2
Typical realizations of RP monophthongs

/ɪ/, as in *pit*
- The lips are loosely spread.
- Older speakers tend to have a closer vowel than younger ones do. The difference between words like *peat* and *pit* for these older speakers is therefore somewhat smaller than is the case for younger speakers.
- There is a tendency for traditional /ɪ/ to be replaced by /ə/ in some unstressed syllables. In general, younger people are more likely to have /ə/, and high status speakers are more likely to have /ɪ/. Environments for this lexical variability are: the first vowel of the endings *-ity* (e.g. *possibility*), *-itive* (e.g. *positive*), *-ily* (e.g. *happily*), *-ate* (e.g. *fortunate*), *-ible* (e.g. *visible*), *-em* (e.g. *problem*); other unstressed syllables *-ess* (e.g. *hopeless*), *-ace* (e.g. *furnace*), *-age* (e.g. *manage*), *-et* (e.g. *bracelet*), *be-* (e.g. *believe*). The ratio of /ɪ/ to /ə/, which varies not only between the different environments listed above but also within them, is too complex to report here.

/ɛ/, as in *pet*
- The lips are loosely spread and slightly wider apart than for /ɪ/.
- An /ɛ/ which is close to cardinal vowel 2, [e], may sometimes be heard amongst older upper-class speakers and those who would use them as models. By the late 1980s, Gimson (1988) had labelled this realization as 'over-refined' while one which forms a glide towards [ə] is perceived as affected; such perceptions continue today.
- Note that the monophthongization of /ɛə/ to [ɛː] in contemporary RP (see section on diphthongs below) means that pairs of words such as *bed* and *bared*, *fez* and *fairs/fares*, or *Ken* and *cairn*, are distinguished solely by the length of the vowel rather than by vowel quality.

/a/, as in *pat*
- The lips are neutrally open.
- Older and more conservative speakers continue to realize /a/ as the closer, fronter vowel [æ], which in some cases may cause listeners to confuse it with /ɛ/. In contemporary RP as spoken by younger speakers the vowel has lowered and retracted somewhat to a quality close to cardinal vowel 4. This tendency to lowering is true also for /ɪ/ and /ɛ/, the changes to all three being part of one process known as a **chain shift** (see Docherty and Watt 2001). As with /ɛ/, a closer realization of /a/ – around cardinal vowel 3 [ɛ], or with a glide towards [ə] – may be perceived by some as refined, but is more likely to be seen as affected or at least old-fashioned by most British people.

- There is lexical variability involving /a/ and /ɑː/, both being used in the following words, amongst others: *plastic, plasticine, photograph, elastic, transfer.*

/ʌ/, as in *putt*
- The lips are neutrally open.
- Older speakers may realize /ʌ/ as a rather more retracted vowel than that indicated in Figure 3.2.

/ɑː/, as in *bard*
- The lips are neutrally open.
- Upper-class speakers may have a more retracted realization, close to cardinal vowel 5 [ɑ].
- Note the lexical variability between /ɑː/ and /a/ referred to above.

/ɒ/, as in *pot*
- There is slight open lip-rounding.
- Among some upper-class and very conservative speakers, lexical variability between /ɒ/ and /ɔː/ is found in words where the vowel precedes /f, s, θ/, as in *off, cross, across, soft, cloth.* These pronunciations are now very rare among RP speakers as a whole, and are generally considered affected.
- In words which have *al* or *au* in the spelling there is also variation between /ɒ/ and /ɔː/, e.g. *salt, fault, Austria,* though again this is now rather uncommon except among more conservative RP speakers.

/ɔː/, as in *board*
- There is medium lip-rounding.
- The great majority of RP speakers use this vowel in words that once were pronounced with [ɔə] (e.g. *court, four, door*). They therefore make no distinction between, for example, *caught* and *court* /kɔːt/ or *pour/pore* and *paw* /pɔː/. Some older speakers maintain the distinction, and so have an extra vowel phoneme /ɔə/. This represents a clear case of systemic variability.
- It is increasingly common for RP speakers also to use /ɔː/ in at least some words in which /ʊə/ has been traditional, for example, *cure, tour, poor, sure.* This can be seen as a case of lexical variability, but the fact that there are so many speakers for whom almost every potential /ʊə/ word is pronounced with /ɔː/ strongly suggests that /ʊə/ has all but lost its phonemic status. Word frequency appears to have a role in the choice of the traditional /ʊə/ over /ɔː/: words such as *dour* and *lure* are on balance more likely to be pronounced with /ʊə/ than are common words like *poor* and *sure. Poor* is thus for many speakers another member of the set of homophones containing *paw, pour,* and *pore.*

/ʊ/, as in *put*
- The lip position for this vowel ranges from close lip-rounding to a neutral lip position.
- There is lexical variability between /ʊ/ and /uː/ in a number of words, including *room* (an individual speaker may have /uː/ in *room* but /ʊ/ in *bathroom*), *groom*, *broom* and *tooth*.
- For many younger RP speakers the vowel has fronted and unrounded to a quality close to [ə]. Some have taken this process so far that /ʊ/ can quite easily be mistaken for /ɪ/: thus *foot* and *fit* can sound very similar (see Torgersen 2002).

/uː/, as in *boot*
- The lips may be closely rounded, but this aspect of the vowel has become quite variable.
- This vowel is rarely any longer fully back or rounded, as per the traditional RP vowel, which was close to cardinal vowel 8 [u]. In contemporary RP, however, the vowel has fronted to a quality closer to [ʉ], and may be markedly diphthongal. The latter sort of pronunciation tends to be characterized by a centralized, often only slightly rounded, onset, as in for example *suit* [sɵʉt].

/ɜː/, as in *bird*
- There is no lip-rounding.
- This vowel varies between open-mid and close-mid.
- Some younger RP speakers, particularly female ones, produce this vowel with a relatively open quality, approaching [ɐː].

/ə/, as in *father***
- There is no lip-rounding.
- Referred to as **schwa**, this vowel is never stressed (except in emphatic pronunciations of words like *the* or *a*)
- In final position, as in *carer*, /ə/ is usually more open than elsewhere (in *regret*, for example).

Diphthongs

There are eight diphthongs in our analysis of RP. Three of these are **centring**, that is, having schwa /ə/ as the second element. The other five diphthongs are **closing**, with the first element in each being more open than the second.

Centring diphthongs
See Figure 3.3 for typical realizations.

/ɪə/, **as in** *beer*

- There is no lip-rounding.

- Associated with upper-class RP (but often perceived as affected) is a second element which is more open than [ə].

- Much more frequent than this, however, is a tendency to monophthongize this vowel by omitting the glide, so that words like *beer* are often heard as [bɪ̝ː], especially when they occur in compounds such as *beer garden*. This smoothing process also applies to /ɛə/ (see below) and /ʊə/, as noted earlier (and see below).

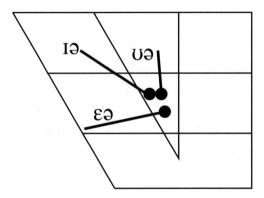

Figure 3.3
Typical
realizations
of RP
centring
diphthongs

/ɛə/, **as in** *bear*

- There is no lip-rounding.

- As discussed under Monophthongs above (p. 48), there is variability between [ɛə] and [ɛː], with the monophthong being favoured by younger speakers, and [ɛə] being perhaps more common in less frequently occurring words in their speech. Thus for an individual speaker, *air* may most often be [ɛː] and *heir* [ɛə].

/ʊə/, **as in** *poor*

- There is some initial lip-rounding.

- As noted above, many speakers have /ɔː/ in words that were traditionally pronounced with /ʊə/.

Closing diphthongs

See Figure 3.4 for typical realizations.

/eɪ/, **as in** *bay*

- The lips are spread.

- The diphthong's starting point varies between close-mid (old-fashioned) and open-mid.

/aɪ/, **as in** *buy*

- The lips are somewhat spread for the second element.

- As with /eɪ/, there is variation in the openness of the first element, but individual speakers will keep the first elements of /eɪ/ and /aɪ/ far enough apart to maintain a distinction.

Figure 3.4
Typical
realizations
of RP
closing
diphthongs

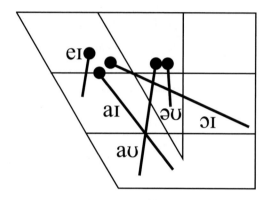

/ɔɪ/, **as in** *boy*

- The lips are rounded for the first element.

/əʊ/, **as in** *boat*

- The lips are somewhat rounded for the second element.

- The first element is usually [ə], though it is increasingly common to hear a quality somewhat fronter than this. For some young RP speakers there is only a small distance between the vowels of *post* and *paste*. Older speakers may retain [o] as the first element, as do some younger speakers when the vowel precedes [ɫ], as in *bowl*.

/aʊ/, **as in** *bout*

- The lips may be somewhat rounded for the second element.

- Some upper-class speakers, including members of the British royal family, have a fronted second element [ɨ], which may cause listeners to confuse the vowel with /aɪ/. Thus one person's *house* may appear to rhyme with another speaker's *mice*.

Closing diphthongs followed by schwa /ə/

All five closing diphthongs may be followed by /ə/ within a word, either as an integral part of the word (e.g. *hire* /haɪə/), or as a suffix, (e.g. *higher* /haɪə/). Such three-element vowels, unsurprisingly, are known as **triphthongs**, although it may be argued that the morpheme boundary in words like *higher* renders them **disyllabic** (having two syllables), which would mean that the /aɪə/ in *higher* is not a triphthong, as per *hire*, but a sequence of a diphthong and a monophthong. However, for our purposes we will treat them as triphthongs.

While all three vowel elements may be maintained in careful or slow speech, in faster speech the second element is usually omitted through smoothing. Some younger speakers carry it further by removing the third element as well, such that triphthongal phonemes are realized as long monophthongs. For these speakers, *tyre*, *tower*, and *tar* are homophones. Monophthongization of this kind seems to be less likely when the schwa represents a suffix. Thus *fire* may more readily become [fɑː] than *flyer* will become [flɑə]. The monophthongized forms are, as we saw for /ɛə/, common in compounds, e.g. *fire brigade* ['fɑː bɹɪɡeɪd], *Tower Bridge* [tɑː 'bɹɪdʒ], *layer cake* ['lɛː keɪk].

Word	'Full' form	Smoothed forms	
tyre	/taɪə/	[tɑə]	[tɑː]
tower	/taʊə/	[taə]	[tɑː]
layer	/leɪə/	[leə]	[lɛː]
slower	/sləʊə/	[sləː]	

Note that for [aə] and [ɑə], the notional difference in the first element of the reduced forms of words like *tyre* and *tower* is so small that the two words (and others like them) have become homophones for many speakers. This reduction of two distinctive sounds into one is referred to as **neutralization**.

[eə] may be neutralized with respect to /ɛə/, so that *layer* and *lair*, for example, may be homophones. Both may be further reduced to [ɛː] (see above), though there is resistance to monophthongization where the schwa represents a suffix. Thus *layer*, as in *layer cake*, is more likely to be realized as [lɛː] than is *layer*, as in *bricklayer*.

[ɔː]: The reduced form of /əʊə/ may be realized as [ɔː], neutralizing the contrast with /ɜː/. Thus *slower* and *slur* may be homophones.

The recordings

The reader of the word list was relatively young at the time of recording and therefore has (WL 15) *bear* /bɛː/ and (WL 42) *poor* /pɔː/. There are three other speakers: two men aged about forty, and a woman of about thirty. All have been to public (i.e. private) school. The first and third speakers would generally be regarded as mainstream RP speakers. The second speaker, however, may be regarded as a marginal RP speaker, since there are features of his speech which might cause other RP speakers to think of him as a near-RP speaker from the south-east of England.

Differences between the speakers

There is no apparent systemic variability between the speakers, but some lexical variability is evident between them:

(a) Speaker 1 has /iː/ and /ɪ/ variably as the final vowel in words like *city* [compare *unfriendly* (l. 6) with *seedy* (l. 14)]. In this he is more conservative than the other two speakers, who have /iː/ throughout.

(b) In the word *if*, Speaker 1 (l. 3) has /v/ rather than the more common /f/ (Speaker 3, l. 33).

(c) Speaker 1 has /a/ as the first vowel in *contrasted* (l. 33). This would usually be an indication of a north of England background, which the speaker does not have. It may be related to carefulness of speech.

Realizational variability

(a) Speaker 2 realizes /aɪ/ with a more retracted initial element than the others.

(b) While all three speakers have a fronted realization of /uː/ (unlike more conservative speakers), Speaker 3 also exhibits very little lip-rounding, at least some of the time.

(c) Speaker 2 exhibits more glottalization than the others. This feature, and his realization of /aɪ/ (see under Diphthongs above), will contribute to some RP speakers possibly considering him to be a near-RP speaker.

(d) Speaker 1 releases plosives in environments in which most speakers would not (e.g. *tacked down*, l. 34). This feature is a marker of careful speech.

(e) Speaker 1 has a noticeably open and back realization of final /ə/ (e.g. *gear*, l. 29).

(f) Speaker 3 has a more fronted first element in /əʊ/.

It is also worth noting the occasional presence of what is called **creaky voice** in the speech of Speaker 3 (e.g. *very thick*, l. 19), which is a not uncommon feature in RP.

Speaker 1

The first speaker talks about the advantages and disadvantages of living in Milton Keynes, where he lives and works. We use 'er' and 'erm' to indicate the filled pauses [ɜː] and [ɜːm], which this speaker and Speaker 2 use frequently.

The advantages are that you don't need a car, there's quite good
shopping, it's been landscaped absolutely superbly, with beautiful
roads, and if you live in any of the houses, you don't know the roads
are there, just because of the way they've built them. Erm, it's new,
5 and it's clean, erm . . . Some of the disadvantages are that the people
are horrible and unfriendly, erm . . . They're brusque and ill-educated
nouveau riche, erm . . . thugs, basically . . . rich, thick thugs . . . erm . . .
who make life really miserable . . . erm . . . on things like the roads,
with a lot of bellyaching and V-signs and insults . . . erm . . . There's
10 quite a lot of unemployment. Certainly, five years ago it had the
highest suicide rate of any city in Britain. I don't know whether that's
still true, erm . . . And it's now old enough for bits of it to be falling apart.
And the bits that are falling apart are doing so in a horrible and really
seedy, ugly way. So there's a lot of, er, depressed and unhappy and
15 very poor people there as well. So you've got, erm . . . it's a kind of
reflection of the nation. You've got . . . er . . . rich with no worries at
all, and deeply poor and ground down.

[The speaker goes on to talk about being burgled twice.]

The first time, I got home, I got off my bike, and everything, and
was actually undoing the front door, and looked at the window,
20 thought, God, I'm sure I didn't leave . . . the venetian blind was all
crooked and bent . . . I can't have left it like that, and I'd actually got
the door unlocked before I even realized what it was that had
occurred, and I went in and there was very little mess, and gradually
I noticed what was missing – the video recorder immediately, but
25 during the course of the evening I kept finding more things that were
no longer there. Erm . . . there were only four things altogether, I
think a video, er, Sony Walkman, erm, and a couple of other things
which I can't remember. But the second occasion was much worse.
Er . . . there was a hell of a mess, erm, with upturned gear, er, all the
30 covers opened and the stuff pulled out, erm, even in the kitchen
where the stuff is very boring . . . erm . . . and everything that had
any value at all seemed to me to have been taken. And very
carefully, which contrasted with the mess. The hi-fi had all its cabling
neatly tacked down, running around the skirting boards. It'd been
35 pulled up incredibly neatly, so that not only did they take the gear
but also all the cabling as well. Er . . . and so far . . . erm . . . the
dealings with the insurance company have been fraught with sort of
misunderstanding and, erm, lack of progress.

Note
A V-sign (l. 9) is a rude gesture made with the index and middle fingers, with
the palm of the hand facing inwards.

Speaker 2

The second speaker describes a motoring accident in which he was involved.

Erm ... I'll tell you a s ... a story about something that ... that happened a couple of years ago. Erm ... I was driving in ... driving in to work one day ... and, er, it was a ... a fairly normal day ... th ... the road was a little bit wet. Erm, other than that there was good
5 visibility ... and I was coming ... er ... in along one of the ... one of the access roads to the, er, university, when, er, a car, a Ford Capri, came towards me, and ... erm ... I realized that this car was about to hit me ... erm ... so I ... I braked quite hard and er ... erm ... stopped. The car hit me quite hard on the ... on the right-hand side
10 ... and ... erm ... my immediate reaction was to make sure that, er, the, er ... the driver of the other car realized that he ... that he was in the ... in the wrong. So I rolled down my window and said to him ... erm ... What ... what the heck do you think you're doing? You've ... you've, er, made a mess of my car. And the ... the driver, who was
15 a young man, apologized and said yes ... erm ... his ... his his brakes, erm, locked and he ... and he skidded on ... on the wet surface. Erm, anyway, it, er, subsequently transpired that this ... this young man in fact worked for a ... a ... a company that repairs cars ... erm ... it ... he'd ... he'd come to the university to collect it ... er,
20 the reason was that, erm, the car was going in to have its brakes fixed ... erm ... so it wasn't surprising perhaps that the brakes locked. It subsequently transpired that the ... the easiest way of, er, transporting my car, which was ... which couldn't be driven away, was for this young man to phone his ... his own company and get the ... the erm
25 ... lorry out that erm ... to get the salvage lorry out. So this ... this happened. The salvage lorry came round, and the erm ... er ... my car was then taken off to the garage, and, erm ... I then thought about it, and talked to my insurance company. Er ... they said yes, it was all right for them to do the repair ... erm ... and which they
30 subsequently did. I ... I reckoned that it'd be quite a good idea to get them to do the repair since ... since they made the ... made the mess in the first place, I was quite likely to have quite a good repair done. And so it was. And, erm ... and in fact I then decided to use the same company to service my car ... and the er ... the man in the, erm ...
35 the ... the owner of the ... of the garage said: 'Well, this isn't the usual way we get customers.'

Speaker 3

The third speaker is a thirty-year-old woman. She describes a visit to the Amazon which she made some years previously.

Erm . . . in the days before husbands and children, erm, I did quite a lot of travelling, and erm . . . one of the th . . . places I went to was to the Amazon. And, erm, I hadn't really . . . it's when I . . . I . . . I knew my husband and, erm . . . then but . . . just as a friend really. And so
5 we, erm, decided that we, or *he* decided that we would go to Brazil and, er, I'd been travelling anyway . . . came back for Christmas, two days to wash my rucksack, and off we went to Rio. And, erm, I hadn't given it any thought at all. And the next thing I knew we went up to, er, Manaus, which is a free port up on the Amazon, where we met
10 some chap who'd got a boat, erm, which was rather like the *African Queen*. Erm . . . and I felt like Katharine Hepburn. And we then, erm, went in this boat up the Amazon and then off up one of the tributaries, erm, where we then came across this little South American tribe, some Indians, erm, who lent us a canoe. So we then left most of
15 our luggage behind and just took a rucksack with a cu . . . with a T-shirt and a toothbrush and a bag of rice and a rifle. And then we had a hammock and a mosquito net, which didn't bode well. And off we went, erm, then w . . . on foot. Erm, it was very wet and, er, oh, we just . . . we . . . and the vegetation was very thick and we . . . you had to . . .
20 we had a guide and a cook and a . . . and another boy . . . and, erm . . . so we went off in our . . . in our canoes and then . . . left those in the side, in some reeds somewhere, and then walked, erm . . . we walked for four days into the jungle. Erm . . . the mosquitoes were appalling, the rain was appalling . . . erm, and we were hungry, and i . . . in four
25 days it was just very interesting that you could feel yourself reverting back to nature . . .

[Interviewer asks if speaker had been in danger at any time.]

Well if . . . yes. I mean there . . . when we first got into the i . . . o . . . actually sort of out of the canoe and into the jungle . . . erm, our guide had er [toe?] . . . had bare feet and he . . . d . . . I mean he didn't speak
30 any, any English at all, but erm . . . suddenly you could see that he just leapt and . . . and you c . . . see the whites of his eyes, and he'd trodden on a deadly poisonous snake, something called a *surucucu*. And he'd've been dead in thirty seconds if it'd bitten him . . . erm, and without him – I mean, he was our guide – and without him we would never have
35 got out again . . . erm, so that was quite dangerous, and . . . I mean who knows what sort of . . . animals were . . . or . . . or reptiles were around at night, and all spiders or whatever.

[Interviewer asks if speaker had seen other forest animals.]

Monkeys, yeah, yeah, and turtles and ... but you know, the vegetation was so ... I mean, it was so thick that ... I mean ... you
40 couldn't see ... I don't know, te ... er ... ten feet in front of you ... and so we we literally had machetes and we we were cutting our way through the ... through the undergrowth ... but the flora and fauna were s ... I mean it was just beautiful ... erm ... yeah, it was a very ... it was a ... an incredible experience really, because it's very
45 unusual in your lives that you're ... or ... in this civilization that we live in ... er, that ... that you ever go without and that you actually are concerned for your ... for your welfare, or and ... that you wonder where your next meal's going to come from.

4 Regional accent variation

As we have already seen, the accent of British English which has been most fully described, and which is usually taught to foreign learners, is the accent known as RP.

In this chapter we first give a brief outline of the main regional differences to be found in accents of British English other than RP, and then compare them with RP. We do not, however, attempt to give a detailed account of all the regional and social differences in pronunciation to be found in British Isles English. In particular, we do not attempt at all to describe accents associated with traditional dialects, spoken by older people in rural areas (for these, see Wakelin 1977). We concentrate instead on urban and other regional accents of the sort most widely heard around Britain and Ireland, and which are most likely to be encountered by visitors from overseas. More detailed discussion of phonological features can be found in Chapter 5. Intonation is also dealt with briefly in cases where it deviates markedly from the general RP-like pattern.

Regional accent differences

The vowel /ʌ/

(a) One of the best-known differences between English accents is one of phoneme inventory – that is, the presence or absence of particular phonemes (see p. 39). Typically, the vowel /ʌ/ does not occur in the accents of the north and midlands of England, and in some accents of the Republic of Ireland. In these accents, /ʊ/ is to be found in those words that elsewhere have /ʌ/. The vowel /ʌ/ is relatively recent in the history of English, having developed by **phonemic split** from the older vowel /ʊ/. Northern English and Irish accents have not taken part in this development. The result is that pairs of words such as *put~putt* or *could~cud*, which are distinguished in Welsh, Scottish, and southern English accents, are not distinguished in the north and midlands of England, where pairs like *blood* and *good* or *mud* and *hood* are perfect rhymes. (There are a few common words, though, which have /ʌ/ in the south of England but which have /ɒ/ in much of the north of England. These include *one* and *none*, both of which rhyme with *gone* rather than *gun* in these areas, and *tongue*, which rhymes with *song* rather than *sung*.)

Many northern English speakers, perhaps under the influence of RP, have a vowel which is between /ʊ/ and /ʌ/ in quality in words such as *but* (and sometimes in words such as *put* as well). Generally, this vowel is around [ə]. This is particularly true of younger, middle-class speakers in areas of the southern midlands. Some speakers too, of course, hypercorrect (see Chapter 1), such that *butcher* might be pronounced ['bʌtʃə].

We can also note that many (particularly older) northern English speakers who lack /ʌ/ have /uː/ rather than /ʊ/ in words such as *hook*, *book*, *look*, *took*, and *cook*. They therefore distinguish pairs such as *book* and *buck*, which in the south are distinguished respectively as /bʊk/ and /bʌk/, as /buːk/ and /bʊk/. All English English accents (i.e. those of England) have shortened the original long /uː/ in <-oo-> words to /ʊ/ in items such as *good* and *hood*, and all seem to have retained /uː/ in words such as *mood* and *food*. But in other cases there is variation: RP speakers may have either /uː/ or /ʊ/ in *room* and *broom*, eastern accents have /ʊ/ rather than /uː/ in *roof* and *hoof*, while western accents, as well as those from parts of Wales, may have /ʊ/ rather than /uː/ in *tooth*, and so on.

(b) In descriptions of RP it is usual to consider /ʌ/ and /ə/ as distinct vowels, as in *butter* /'bʌtə/. This also holds good for accents of the south-east of England, Ireland, and Scotland. However, speakers from many parts of Wales, western England, and the midlands (as well as some northern speakers – see above) have vowels that are identical in both cases: *butter* /'bətə/, *another* /ə'nəðə/ (see Table 4.1).

Table 4.1 /ʌ/, /ʊ/ and /ə/

	but	put
RP	/ʌ/	/ʊ/
Northern England	/ʊ/	/ʊ/
Western England; modified northern I	/ə/	/ʊ/
Modified northern II	/ə/	/ə/
Hypercorrect northern	/ʌ/	/ʌ/

/a/ and /ɑː/

Another very well-known feature which distinguishes northern from southern English English accents concerns the vowels /a/ and /ɑː/. In discussing this feature we have to isolate a number of different classes of words:

(1) *pat, bad, cap, can, gas, land*   RP /pat/, etc.

(2) *path, laugh, grass*   RP /pɑːθ/, etc.

(3) *dance, grant, demand*   RP /dɑːns/, etc.

(4) *part, bar, cart*   RP /pɑːt/, etc.

(5) *half, palm, banana, can't*   RP /hɑːf/, etc.

RP has /a/ in set (1), and /ɑː/ in all other sets. This incidence of vowels in the different sets is also found in all south-eastern English and in many southern Irish accents. In the midlands and north of England, on the other hand, words in sets (2) and (3) have the vowel /a/ rather than /ɑː/, although they do have /ɑː/ in the classes of (4) and (5). Thus, whereas southerners say /gɹɑːs/ *grass* and /gɹɑːnt/ *grant*, northerners say /gɹas/ and /gɹant/.

This difference between the north and south of England is due to the fact that the original short vowel /a/ was lengthened in the south of England (a) before the voiceless fricatives /f, θ, s/, and (b) before certain consonant clusters containing an initial /n/ or /m/. Change (a) affected most words in southern English accents, though there are numerous exceptions, such as *daffodil, gaff, Jaffa, raffle, Catherine, maths* (but *afterm*[ɑː]*th*), *ass, crass, gas, hassle, lass, mass, chassis,* and *tassel,* which have /a/ in RP and southern accents. There are also some words which vary: some southerners have /a/ in *graph, photograph,* and *alas,* while others have /ɑː/.

Change (b) is rather more complex, and less complete. We can note the following phonological contexts, and typical southern English pronunciations:

	/ɑː/		/a/
– nt	*plant*	but	*pant*
– ns	*dance*	but	*romance*
– nʃ*	*branch*	but	*mansion*
– nd	*demand*	but	*band*
– mp	*example*	but	*camp*

* Many speakers have [tʃ] rather than [ʃ] here. (Words such as *transport, plastic* can have either /a/ or /ɑː/.)

Some Welsh and Irish accents, like many Australian accents, have change (a) but not change (b): they have /gɹɑːs/ *grass* but /dans/ *dance.*

This discussion of the incidence of /a/ and /ɑː/ in words like *grass* and *dance* is not relevant to Scottish and northern Irish accents (except for some RP-influenced accents – that used by middle-class Edinburgh speakers, for example). These accents do not have the /a/~/ɑː/ contrast, having /a/ not only in sets (1), (2) and (3), but also in sets (4) and (5).

(The /a/ may be pronounced [æ], [a], [ɐ] or [ɑ] in these varieties.) Pairs such as *palm ~ Pam* and *calm ~ cam* are therefore homophones.

This is also true of those accents most typical of the south-west of England (see Map 4.1). RP speakers in this area do, of course, have the /a/ ~ /ɑː/ contrast, as do many other middle-class speakers whose accents resemble RP. But speakers with more strongly regional south-western accents do not have the contrast, or at most have a contrast that is variable or doubtful. It is certain that south-western accented speakers have /a/ (often pronounced [aˑ]) in words of classes (1), (2) and (3) (for class (4) see below). The doubt lies in what these speakers do with words of set (5). Typically, it seems, words such as *father*, *half* and *can't* have /a/. Words such as *palm* and *calm* often retain the /l/, and generally have /ɑ/, as in /pɑlm/. More recent loan words like *banana*, *gala* and *tomato*, which have /ɑː/ in south-eastern and northern English accents and /a/ in Northern Ireland and Scotland, most typically have /a/ but *may* have /ɑː/, and are even pronounced [təˈmɑːɹtəʊ], etc., by some speakers from western England.

/ɪ/ and /iː/

Another major north/south differentiating feature involves the final vowel of words like *city*, *money*, *coffee* (as well as unstressed forms of *me*, *he*,

Map 4.1
Distribution
of /a/ and /ɑː/
in British
English

we). In most parts of northern England these items have /ɪ/, as in /ˈsɪtɪ/ *city*. In the south of England, on the other hand, these words have /iː/, as in /ˈsɪtiː/. The dividing line between north and south is in this case a good deal further north than in the case of the previous two features, with only Cheshire, Lancashire and Yorkshire and areas to the north being involved – except that, again, Liverpool in this case patterns with the southern rather than the northern accents. Tyneside and Humberside also have /iː/ rather than /ɪ/.

Scottish accents typically have the same vowel in this final position as they have in words such as *gate* or *face*, so that e.g. *racy* is [ˈɾese]. Accents of the Republic of Ireland typically have /iː/.

/ɹ/

All English accents permit /ɹ/ where it occurs *before* a vowel, as in *rat*, *trap*, *carry*. They vary, however, in whether they permit the pronunciation of /ɹ/ after a vowel (**post-vocalic** /ɹ/), as in words such as *bar*, *bark*, *firm*, *butter*, etc. RP does not have post-vocalic /ɹ/, so for these words has /baː/, /baːk/, /fɜːm/ and /ˈbʌtə/. Scottish and Irish accents (like most North American accents) do, conversely, have /ɹ/ in this position. These /ɹ/-pronouncing accents are known as rhotic accents; those which do not permit post-vocalic /ɹ/ are called non-rhotic accents. Beyond the UK, non-rhotic accents can be found in many parts of the world, including Australia, New Zealand, South Africa, the southern United States, New York City, and the Caribbean.

Within England and Wales the position of post-vocalic /ɹ/ in regional accents is quite complex, but we can generalize and say that /ɹ/-ful pronunciations are being lost – post-vocalic /ɹ/, in other words, is dying out – and that one is more likely to hear post-vocalic /ɹ/ in the speech of older, working-class rural speakers than from younger middle-class urban speakers. Map 4.2 shows those areas where post-vocalic /ɹ/ still occurs in the British Isles.

This difference between English accents is due to a linguistic change involving the loss of post-vocalic /ɹ/, which began some centuries ago in the south-east of England, and has since spread to other regions. This loss of /ɹ/ has had a further consequence (see also p. 46). The consonant /ɹ/ was lost in these accents before a following consonant, as in *cart*, but was retained before a following vowel, as in *carry*. This meant that whether or not the /ɹ/ was pronounced in words like *car* depended on whether it was followed by a word beginning with a vowel or a word beginning with a consonant (or by a pause). Thus we have

	car alarm	with /ɹ/	/ˈkaːɹəˈlaːm/
but	*car keys*	without /ɹ/	/ˈkaːˈkiːz/

Map 4.2
Post-vocalic
/ɹ/ in the UK
and Ireland

A = post-vocalic /ɹ/ present
B = post-vocalic /ɹ/ absent

The /ɹ/ in the pronunciation of *car alarm* is known as linking /ɹ/, as we saw earlier. Originally, we can assume, what happened was that speakers deleted (or failed to pronounce) the /ɹ/ before a following consonant. Subsequently, however, this pattern has for most speakers been restructured, analogically, so that it is now interpreted in such a way that /ɹ/ is inserted before a following vowel. This means that analogous to:

soar /sɔː/   *soar up* /sɔːɹ ʌp/

we now also have:

draw /dɹɔː/   *draw up* /dɹɔːɹ ʌp/

It will be recalled that an /ɹ/ which occurs in the latter position – i.e. in cases where there is no <r> in the spelling (which of course reflects the original pronunciation) – is known as intrusive /ɹ/. Because there is no <r> in the spelling, intrusive /ɹ/ has often been frowned upon by schoolteachers and others as being 'incorrect'. However, it is now quite normal in non-rhotic accents of English in the UK, and even in RP it is quite usual for speakers to say:

idea [ɹ] *of*	*Shah* [ɹ] *of Iran*	*Hannah* [ɹ] *is*
draw [ɹ] *it*	*china* [ɹ] *ornament*	*pizza* [ɹ] *and chips*

We can say that where one of the vowels /ɑː ɔː ɜː ɪə ɛə ə/ occurs before another vowel, an /ɹ/ is automatically inserted. This process is so automatic that speakers are usually unaware that they do it. Generally, too, we can say that the tendency is now so widespread that if speakers with a south-eastern-type English accent fail to use intrusive /ɹ/, especially after /ə/ or /ɪə/, they are probably not native speakers. Some RP speakers carefully avoid the use of intrusive /ɹ/ *within* words, and will not say *drawing* /'dɹɔːɹɪŋ/, as many other non-RP speakers do. The stigma attached to intrusive /ɹ/ is, however, receding. Many younger RP speakers appear to have no objection to it whatsoever, and express surprise when it is pointed out to them that some people consider it incorrect or ugly (see also p. 46, and Foulkes 1998 for further discussion).

Accents such as those of Scotland which have preserved post-vocalic /ɹ/ do not, of course, have intrusive /ɹ/ (the analogical process does not apply), and Scottish speakers often observe that 'English speakers say *India* /'ɪndɪəɹ/'. English speakers, in fact, do not normally say /'ɪndɪəɹ/ if the word is uttered on its own, but they *do* pronounce the word this way if it is in a phrase such as /'ɪndɪəɹ ən pɑːkɪ'stɑːn/ *India and Pakistan*.

Loss of post-vocalic /ɹ/ in RP and many other accents also means that many words, such as *butter*, *better*, or *hammer*, end in -/ə/ (rather than -/əɹ/). When new words such as *America*, *china*, *banana*, or *algebra* were adopted into English, there was in these accents therefore no problem. They fitted into the same pattern and were pronounced with final /ə/ – (with intrusive /ɹ/, of course, if the next word began with a vowel). However, in accents where post-vocalic /ɹ/ was preserved, there were no words other than proper names, such as *Hannah* or *Noah*, that ended in -/ə/. The problem therefore arose of how to incorporate these new words into the sound structures of these particular varieties. In many Scottish accents the solution seems to have been to end words such as these with /a/ (the same vowel as in *hat*): /'tʃaɪna/ *china*. In accents in the west of England, on the other hand, another solution was sometimes adopted and the new words assimilated to the pattern of *butter*. We therefore find, in towns such as Southampton, pronunciations such as /bə'nɑːnəɹ/ *banana*, /və'nɪləɹ/ *vanilla*, and so on. (This is not the same phenomenon as intrusive /ɹ/, because in these accents the /ɹ/ occurs even where there is a following consonant.) In Bristol, the solution was to assimilate them to the pattern of *bottle* and *apple* /'apəl/. This is the so-called 'Bristol /l/' (see pp. 81–2), as in *America* /ə'mɛɹɪkəl/, *Eva* /'iːvəl/, and so on. A similar, but wholly independent, phenomenon is also reported for south-east Pennsylvania English (Gick 2002).

Note that the actual pronunciation of /ɹ/ also varies quite widely. In Scotland, Wales and northern England a frequent pronunciation is the alveolar tap [ɾ]; in the south-west of England, in the Highlands of Scotland, and in Ireland a retroflex approximant [ɻ] is used; and in south-eastern England the usual form is the alveolar approximant [ɹ] also usual in RP. The alveolar trill [r] is stereotypical of Scottish English, and although it is used in many accents around Scotland, it is relatively infrequent (see pp. 102, 106). Other variants include the uvular fricative [ʁ] in rural north-east England, and labio-dental [ʋ] from younger speakers principally in the south of England. See also Chapter 5.

/uː/ and /ʊ/

We have already noted that Scottish and Northern Irish accents have no distinction between /a/ and /ɑː/. The same is also true, for the most part, of the similar pairs of vowels /ʊ/ and /uː/, and /ɒ/ and /ɔː/.

Thus Scottish speakers make no distinction between pairs of words such as the following:

Pam	~	*palm*
pull	~	*pool*
cot	~	*caught*

/h/

Unlike RP, most urban regional accents of England and Wales do not have /h/, or are at least variable in its usage. For speakers of these accents, therefore, pairs like *art* and *heart* or *arm* and *harm* are pronounced the same way. /h/ is retained in accents of the north-east of England such as that of Newcastle, although it disappears quickly as one travels southwards: /h/-dropping is reported for Sunderland, and it is virtually categorical in Middlesbrough and other parts of Teesside. Scottish and Irish accents, on the other hand, do not feature H-dropping.

[ʔ]

RP speakers may use the glottal stop (see pp. 42–3) word-initially before vowels, as in [ʔant] *ant,* or before certain consonants or consonant clusters, e.g. [baʔtʃ] *batch,* [sɪʔks] *six,* [ˈsɪmʔplɪ] *simply* (Brown 1990; Fabricius 2002; Altendorf 2003).

In most British regional accents, however, the glottal stop is more widely used, particularly as an allophone of word-medial and word-final /t/. It is most common in the speech of younger urban working-class speakers, and is now found in almost all regions of the UK, with the particular exception of many parts of Wales and northern Scotland. It occurs much more frequently in some phonological contexts than others:

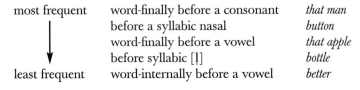

most frequent	word-finally before a consonant	*that man*
	before a syllabic nasal	*button*
	word-finally before a vowel	*that apple*
	before syllabic [l]	*bottle*
least frequent	word-internally before a vowel	*better*

As noted in Chapter 1, it appears that many younger RP speakers are also adopting [ʔ] in some of the above contexts, despite (or perhaps because of) the stigma of ugliness, inarticulacy and 'sloppiness' that is often attached to the form. The fact that prominent public figures, such as the prime minister, Tony Blair, and certain younger members of the British royal family, can be heard to use glottal stops in pre-consonantal, pre-nasal and even word-final pre-vocalic positions suggests that this stigma may be receding, however.

In some areas, especially the north-east of England, East Anglia, Northern Ireland, and north-eastern Scotland, the glottal stop may also be pronounced simultaneously with the voiceless stops /p, t, k/ in certain positions, most strikingly when between vowels:

flipper	[ˈflɪp͡ʔə(ɹ)]
city	[ˈsɪt͡ʔiː]
flicker	[ˈflɪk͡ʔə(ɹ)]

/ŋ/

(a) Most non-RP speakers of English, particularly when using informal styles, do not have /ŋ/ in the suffix *-ing*. In forms of this type they have /n/ instead:

singing	/ˈsɪŋɪn/
walking	/ˈwɔːkɪn/

This pronunciation has also been stereotypically associated (see also p. 44) with older members of the aristocracy, who are often caricatured as being particularly interested in *huntin', shootin', and fishin'*.

It should be noted that although this habit is popularly termed 'dropping [g]s', it is a process of simple substitution of /n/ for /ŋ/, as nothing is dropped or omitted. It is also important to remember that the phenomenon applies only to /ŋ/ where it occurs in the *–ing* suffix: /ŋ/ in words like *sing* (or *sang, singer, finger*) is never replaced by /n/ in any accent.

(b) In an area of western central England which includes Birmingham, Manchester and Liverpool, words which elsewhere have /ŋ/ and are spelled with <ng> are pronounced with [ŋg], a sequence which has been labelled the 'velar nasal plus':

singer	[ˈsɪŋgə] (rhymes with [ˈfɪŋgə] *finger* and [ˈlɪŋgə] *linger*)
thing	[θɪŋg]

/j/-dropping

At an earlier stage in the history of English, words like *rude* and *rule* were, it is thought, pronounced /ɹjuːd/ and /ɹjuːl/. In modern English, however, the /j/, where it occurred after /ɹ/, has been lost, and the words are now pronounced /ɹuːd/ and /ɹuːl/. The same thing is true of earlier /juː/ after /l/: the name *Luke*, for instance, which formerly had /j/, is today pronounced /luːk/ (except that some – particularly Scottish – accents still preserve /j/ in words like *illumine* and *allude*). /j/ has also been substantially lost after /s/: *suitable* still contains /j/ for most RP speakers, and some older, very conservative RP speakers may retain /j/ in *suit*, but pronunciations like *super* /ˈsjupə/ have long been considered comically old-fashioned (see p. 46). In RP and many other English accents, though, this is as far as the process has gone, and /j/ can still occur before /uː/ after most other consonants.

In certain regional accents, however, the change has progressed a good deal further. In parts of the north of England, for example, /j/ has been lost after /θ/, so that *enthuse* may be /ɛnˈθuːz/. In London, /j/ is very often absent after /n/, so *news* may be /nuːz/ rather than the RP-type /njuːz/. Additionally, as in a number of North American accents, /j/ can also, at least in northern areas of London, be lost after /t/ and /d/, giving *tune* /tuːn/ and *duke* /duːk/ rather than /tjuːn/ and /djuːk/, as in RP.

In a large area of eastern England, however, /j/ has been lost before /uː/ after *all* consonants. This area covers Norfolk and parts of Suffolk, Essex, Cambridgeshire, Northamptonshire, Bedfordshire, Leicestershire, Lincolnshire and Nottinghamshire, and includes the cities of Norwich, Ipswich, Cambridge and Peterborough. In this area pronunciations such as *pew* /puː/, *beauty* /ˈbuːtiː/, *view* /vuː/, *few* /fuː/, *queue* /kuː/, *music* /ˈmuːzɪk/ and *human* /ˈhuːmən/ are quite usual.

Long mid diphthonging

Accents in the south-eastern and southern-central part of England have undergone a process known as **long mid diphthonging** (see Wells 1982). This means that the vowels of *gate* and *boat* have a diphthongal character. Diphthongs may range from [æi] in *gate* and [ʌʉ] in *boat* in London and the south, through [ɛi] and [ɔu], to [ei] and [ou] in the north of the affected area. That is, the more southerly the accent, the wider the diphthong. In local accents elsewhere in the British Isles – the far south-west of England, the far north of England, Wales, Scotland, and Ireland – these vowels have retained older, monophthongal pronunciations such as [geːt] and [boːt].

Regional accent classification

To summarize the contents of this chapter, we can point out that the way in which most of the features we have been discussing are regionally distributed makes it possible to construct a classification of the major accent types to be found within the British Isles. This is illustrated in Map 4.3, which shows accents of English divided into their main divisions and subdivisions, although note must be taken of the fact that the drawing of regional linguistic boundaries is a notoriously difficult and somewhat arbitrary task, and cases could certainly be made for different classifications from those we have used here. Note also that the political frontiers between Northern Ireland and the Republic of Ireland, between Scotland and England, and between England and Wales, do not coincide exactly with accent classification boundaries.

Map 4.3 on p. 70 shows a division of English accents into five major groups in the British Isles: the south of England; the north of England; Wales; the south of Ireland; and Scotland and the north of Ireland. To help clarify the geographical positions of the subdivisions of the north of England and south of England groups, note the position of urban areas as follows:

North-east:	Newcastle, Sunderland, Durham, Middlesbrough
Central north:	Lancaster, York, Bradford, Leeds
Central Lancashire:	Blackburn, Burnley, Accrington
Merseyside:	Liverpool, Birkenhead
Humberside:	Scunthorpe, Hull, Grimsby
North-west Midlands:	Manchester, Derby, Stoke-on-Trent, Chester
East Midlands:	Nottingham, Leicester, Grantham
West Midlands:	Walsall, Birmingham, Wolverhampton, Coventry
South Midlands:	Bedford, Northampton, Milton Keynes
East south-west:	Bristol, Gloucester
West south-west:	Plymouth, Exeter
South-east:	London, Brighton, Dover, Reading
East Anglia:	Norwich, Ipswich

The five south of England areas (the western south-west, the eastern south-west, the south-east, the south Midlands, and East Anglia) are distinguished by having the vowel /ʌ/ in words like *putt* and *cud*. Within the southern area, the two south-western areas are distinguished by having /ɹ/ in *bar* and *bark*, and by lacking the distinction between /a/ and /ɑː/ (see above). They are distinguished from each other by the absence

Map 4.3
Accent
groups of
the British
Isles

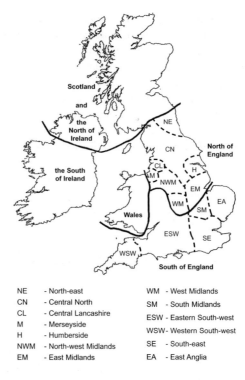

NE	- North-east	WM	- West Midlands
CN	- Central North	SM	- South Midlands
CL	- Central Lancashire	ESW	- Eastern South-west
M	- Merseyside	WSW	- Western South-west
H	- Humberside	SE	- South-east
NWM	- North-west Midlands	EA	- East Anglia
EM	- East Midlands		

of long mid diphthonging in the western south-west. East Anglia has preserved initial /h/, and both East Anglia and the south Midlands have complete /j/-dropping.

Accents in the north of England are distinguished by lacking the vowel /ʌ/ in *putt*, having /ʊ/ in both *putt* and *put*. As can be seen from the map, the north of England area is divided up into eight sub-areas. These are characterized by the following features:

(a) /h/ is preserved in the north-east (but not Teesside or Wearside)

(b) Words such as *singer* are pronounced with /ŋg/ in central Lancashire, Merseyside, the north-west Midlands, and the West Midlands

(c) Postvocalic /ɹ/ is preserved in central Lancashire

(d) Words like *money* have final /iː/ in the north-east, Humberside, Merseyside, and west Midlands areas

(e) Long mid diphthonging in *gate* and *coat* occurs in Merseyside, the north-west Midlands, the east Midlands and the west Midlands (just as it does in the south of England), although it has been spreading into other areas of England in recent decades

(f) /j/-dropping is found in the east Midlands

Ireland and Scotland lack long mid diphthonging; they preserve /h/ and post-vocalic /ɹ/; and, like the south of England, they have /ʌ/ in *putt*. The north of Ireland and Scotland also lack the distinctions between /ʊ/ and /uː/, /a/ and /ɑː/, and /ɒ/ and /ɔː/.

Wales is distinguished by lacking /h/, postvocalic /ɹ/, and long mid diphthonging (though this can be heard in urban south Wales). Welsh accents also have /iː/ in *money*, /ʌ/ in *putt*, and /a/ in *path* (though see Chapter 5).

For the summary of these facts, see Table 4.2.

	/ʌ/ in mud	/ɑː/ in path	/ɑː/ in palm	/iː/ in hazy	/ɹ/ in bar	/ʊ/ in pull	/h/ in harm	/g/ in sing	/j/ in few	[eɪ] in gate
Scotland & N. Ireland	+	−	−	−	+	−	+	−	+	−
S. Ireland	+	+	+	+	+	+	+	−	+	−
Northeast	−	−	+	+	−	+	+	−	+	−
Central north	−	−	+	−	−	+	−	−	+	−
Central Lancs.	−	−	+	−	+	+	−	+	+	−
Merseyside	−	−	+	+	−	+	−	+	+	+
Humberside	−	−	+	+	−	+	−	−	+	−
NW. Midlands	−	−	+	−	−	+	−	+	+	+
E. Midlands	−	−	+	−	−	+	−	−	−	+
W. Midlands	−	−	+	+	−	+	−	+	+	+
S. Midlands	+	+	+	+	−	+	−	−	−	+
E. South-west	+	−	−	+	+	+	−	−	+	+
W. South-west	+	−	−	+	+	+	−	−	+	−
South-east	+	+	+	+	−	+	−	−	+	+
East Anglia	+	+	+	+	−	+	+	−	−	+
Wales	+	−	+	+	−	+	−	−	+	−

Table 4.2 Key phonological characteristics of accents of English in the British Isles

5 British Isles accents and dialects

In this chapter we look in greater detail at the speech of sixteen different areas of the British Isles. These correspond to the sixteen recordings of conversations on the CD available with the book. The speakers on the CD have quite distinct accents, and have been chosen to provide a sample of regional variation which is linguistically and geographically representative. The towns and cities from which the first thirteen speakers come are: **London** (the speech and the speakers being known colloquially as 'Cockney'); **Norwich** (East Anglia); **Bristol** (the west of England); **Pontypridd** (south Wales); **Walsall** (West Midlands); **Leicester** (East Midlands); **Bradford** (Yorkshire); **Liverpool** (Merseyside); **Edinburgh** (central Scotland); **Aberdeen** (north-east Scotland); **Belfast** (Northern Ireland); **Dublin** (eastern Republic of Ireland) and **Galway** (western Republic of Ireland). We also investigate the English of three speakers of traditional dialects (see p. 33) from the mainly rural county of **Devon** in south-west England, from **Northumberland** in the far north of England, and from the **Lowlands of Scotland** (that area lying between and around Glasgow and Edinburgh, but also extending up the east coast of Scotland to Fife, Angus and Aberdeenshire). The locations of these areas are shown on the map on the inside back cover.

We treat each area in turn, indicating first the principal distinguishing features of the particular accent, and making reference where possible to examples of them in the recording (identified by line number in the transcript, e.g. l. 10). This is followed by an orthographic transcription of the relevant recording, and notes on interesting grammatical and lexical features which appear in the recording.

We should point out here, perhaps, that the recordings were not made by actors or in a studio. For the most part they are of people talking with friends in their own homes. In order to obtain 'natural' speech, we wanted the speakers to feel comfortable and relaxed, and to speak as they usually would in friendly conversation. We think that in general we have achieved this. Some of the recordings date back to well before the publication of the first edition of this book in 1979, however, and the conditions in which the recordings were made does mean that there is sometimes considerable background noise, and there are occasions when speakers get excited, are interrupted, turn away from the microphone, or rattle a teacup in its saucer, and for this reason it is not always absolutely clear what has been said. The recordings have been digitally remastered for the current edition of the book and some recordings have been electronically filtered so as to reduce the levels of background noise, but there are limits to how much noise can be removed without affecting the intelligibility of the speaker's voice, or otherwise creating distracting changes in the sound quality.

The recording for each of the first thirteen areas begins with the reading of a word list designed to bring out the principal differences between British Isles accents. For comparison, the very first recording on the CD is of an RP speaker reading the list. The list, together with the RP pronunciation of it, is given in the table on p. xi (and is referred to subsequently as WL, with the number identifying the word, e.g. WL 5).

In the following sections we will repeatedly want to talk about the qualities of different vowels. In working-class London speech ('Cockney'), for example, although the vowel /ʌ/, as in *cup*, is to be found in the same set of words as it is in RP, its realization – that is, the actual sound made – is consistently different from the equivalent RP vowel. To show these differences (which, of course, can be heard on the CD) we make use of vowel charts of the kind introduced in Chapter 3.

1 London

Map 5.1

1.1 The traditional working-class London accent informally termed 'Cockney' is, of course, a southern accent.

  (a) /ʊ/ and /ʌ/ are both present and distinguish between, for example, *put* and *putt* (WL 4, 5; see pp. 59–60). /ʌ/ is realized as [ɐ] (Figure 5.1, a clear example being *blood*, l. 10).

(b) /a/ and /ɑː/ are distributed as in RP (WL 21–6; see pp. 60–2). /a/ is realized as [ɛ̞], or as a diphthong, [ɛi] (Figure 5.1; WL 21; *bag*, l. 35).

(c) Unlike RP, the final vowel of *city*, etc., is /iː/ and not /ɪ/ (WL 19, 20).

1.2 /h/ is almost invariably absent. When it is present, it is likely to be in a stressed position (*happened*, l. 26).

1.3 The glottal stop, [ʔ], is extremely common in London speech. As well as in the environments in which it occurs in RP, it is also found:

(a) accompanying /p/ between vowels (*paper*, l. 2)

(b) representing /t/ between vowels and before a pause (WL 1–6 etc.; *butterfly*, l. 18; *wet*, l. 3).

1.4 (a) The contrast between /θ/ and /f/ is variably lost through the process, known as **TH-fronting**, which collapses the distinction between labio-dental and dental fricatives (see p. 43):

initially	*thin*	/fɪn/
medially	*Cathy*	/kafiː/
finally	*both*	/bəʊf/

(b) Similarly, the contrast between /ð/ and /v/ is also often lost:

medially	*together*	/təˈgɛvə/ (l. 20)
finally	*bathe*	/beɪv/

Initially, /d/ or zero is more likely to be heard for /ð/:

e.g.   *the* (l. 4) is /d/
        they (l. 11) is /eɪ/

Figure 5.1
Phonetic qualities of certain London vowels

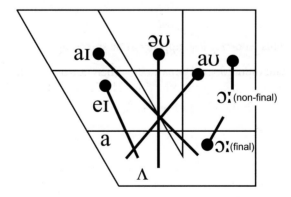

1.5 (a) When /ɔː/ is final it is realized much as the vowel of *pore* in some RP speech; when /ɔː/ is non-final, its realization is much closer, at [oː] (Figure 5.1; cf. WL 45, 48).

(b) As a result of this difference, a distinction (which is absent in RP) is made in the speech of London and of areas to the south of the city, between pairs of words like:

paws [pɔəz] and *pause* [poːz] (WL 48, 49)
bored [bɔəd] and *board* [boːd]

The distinction is made on the basis of the presence or absence of a **morpheme boundary** (i.e. whether there's an inflectional ending on the word). Where, for example, plural, third person singular, or genitive -*s* is added to a word-final /ɔː/, [ɔə] is still found, rather than [ɔː].

1.6 (a) When /l/ occurs finally after a vowel, e.g. *Paul* (WL 30), *well* (l. 18); before a consonant in the same syllable, e.g. *milk*; or as a syllable in itself, e.g. *table*, it is realized as a vowel. Thus: [poʊ, wɛʊ, mɪʊk, ˈtæɪbʊ] (note that the quality of this vowel can vary somewhat – [ɤ] and [o] are also possible). When the preceding vowel is /ɔː/, there may be complete loss of /l/. Thus *Paul's* may be [poːz], i.e. identical with *pause*.

These comments on /l/ are true not only for London but also for the Home Counties, i.e. those counties adjoining London, and it is a feature which seems to be spreading.

(b) The vowels which represent /l/ can alter the quality of the vowels preceding them in such a way as to make homonyms of pairs like:

pool	*pull*	(WL 28, 29)
doll	*dole*	(cf. *doll*, *pole*, WL 31, 29)
peal	*pill*	

This tendency also appears to be spreading.

1.7 Certain diphthongs are markedly different from RP in their realizations (compare Figure 5.1 with Figures 3.3 and 3.4).

(a) /eɪ/ is [æɪ] (WL 40; *paper*, l. 2)

(b) /əʊ/ is [ʌʉ] (WL 12; *soaked*, l. 9)

(c) /aɪ/ is [ɑɪ] (WL 9; *inside*, l. 3)

(d) /aʊ/ may be [æə] (*surrounded*, l. 52), and may trigger intrusive /ɹ/ insertion (see p. 46) as in *how* [ɹ] *about* or *now he* (l. 55).

1.8 -*ing* is /ɪn/:

(a) *laying*, (l. 1, 51) (see p. 67)

(b) In *nothing, something*, etc., *-ing* may be pronounced [ɪŋk] (*anything*, l. 5)

1.9   Initial /p, t, k/ are heavily aspirated, and more so than in RP. In the case of /t/, there is affrication (the tongue tip/blade leave the alveolar ridge slowly, so that [s] is produced before the vowel begins). Thus *tea*, l. 5, is [tsɪi].

1.10   The labio-dental approximant [ʋ] can also be heard in the recording (e.g. *reading*, l. 2, *radiators*, l. 6). This pronunciation has been a feature of London English for some time (see Foulkes and Docherty 2000) but has in recent decades spread widely throughout England. It can be heard in some of the other recordings on the CD.

The recording

The speaker is a working man of about fifty who has lived all his life in London. His accent is quite strong, though certain features, such as the use of /f/ for /θ/, are not so obvious. He is talking about his time in hospital just before his release after an operation.

The reader of the word list is younger, and her accent is not as strong as that of the older male speaker. Notice the variability in the realization of final /t/, which is sometimes [ʔ] and sometimes [t].

I came back to the bed, like, after breakfast. I was just like laying on it a little bit and reading the . . . the paper. And I don't know, I thought suddenly I feel wet in my pyjamas. And I looked inside, and put my hand in. I . . . it is wet. Well, how . . . how the dickens? I ain't spilt any
5   tea or anything down there. So I thought well, I know, I'll go out in the ablution place, like, there . . . they've got some little radiators, all little individual places got a little radiator, put my pyjamas on there to dry, I just thought it was some water. Of course, when I got out there the dressing that was on me, that was soaked in a . . . yeah, like a . . . a
10   watery blood. So, of course I went and saw the sister, and er . . . they put another dressing on it. They put another dressing on it . . . it wasn't . . . wasn't long before that was soaked and all, Fred. Wasn't long before that was soaked. So of course I went and had another one done. So I said to the . . . the nurse, I said . . . guessed to what it was,
15   it was like where they . . . they'd taken the tubes out, and I said to her, 'Have they opened up?' She said, 'No, there's nothing, like o . . . a . . . actually open, it's seeping.' It was seeping through, yeah. Well . . . I said, well, I said, 'If you put s . . . some, like, little butterfly stitches over that first of all . . . out of . . . er . . . er . . . plaster, like, you know
20   . . . hold that together first of all, then put a dressing and a big plaster

on it,' so she done that. But it still didn't . . . yeah, it still seeps through.
And of course I'm going to get worried, and when . . . when she done
it, like, the third time . . . took if off, I'm laying there, I could see it, it
was running away from me like tears. But yeah . . . but anyway . . .
25 yeah . . . well, that's what I said. And of course, what . . . what had
happened, also, that was the Saturday, wasn't it? Yeah, I, er . . . had
my pyjamas. I'd . . . I'd just changed my pyjamas. So I said to Rene, I
phoned Rene there, and I said, 'Could you bring me another one of
my old pairs of pyjamas?' I said, cos, I said, some stain had come
30 through it, you know, how . . . round the waistband and that. So she
brought me in a new pair of 'jamas in the afternoon. I went and
changed them and . . . and that. But blimey, before she went home,
they were worse than the other pair, weren't they? It'd come through
and it had soaked right through and down the leg, and the other pair
35 had dried off a bit in the bag so I thought, well, I'll have to keep them,
so . . . I did get it done again and, er . . . I changed into pyjamas. Well,
of course when it come to the Sunday, I'm going home Sunday, made
arrangements for . . . she's going to pick me up about ten. So of course
I had to see the . . . the sister, and, er . . . she said, 'I'd like the doctor
40 to see that.' Well, time's going on, so I phoned Rene in the morning
and said, 'Don't pick me up at ten, make it nearer twelve,' sort of thing
. . . it'd give me a chance. And, er, anyway, it was . . . was a long while
before this doctor come up. It was only, like, the young one, see,
weekend one. But anyway, the sister, she was getting a bit worried.
45 She said, 'He don't seem to be coming.' So she had a look, and she
said, well, if it was my decision she wouldn't let me home. And, er . . .
yeah, I more or less pleaded with her. I said, 'Well, they're coming
here in a little while.' I said, 'If you'd've told me before,' I said,
'I would have made arrangements and cancelled it.' Anyway, she
50 was still worried, so she went and she found this young doctor.
He come along . . . still laying there, you know, on my bed, sort of
thing, surrounded . . . Eventually he comes ten to twelve, and he
has a look and . . . he's, like, with the nurse there, he wasn't with the
sister. But anyway he said, er . . . 'Well,' he said, 'it don't seem to
55 be weeping now.' He said, 'I don't think it'll weep any more,' he
said, erm . . . he said, 'Well, I'm going to let you go home,' and he
said, er, he said, 'they'll have to be dressed twice a day,' he said.
And, er, he said, 'Twice a day,' he said, 'while it's . . . comes away a
bit wet,' he said, 'and once a day', he said, 'when it's dry,' sort of
60 thing.

Notes

1   The past tense of **come** is variably *came*, e.g. l. 1, and *come* e.g. l. 37, 43, 51
     (see p. 26).

2   The past tense of the full verb **do** is *done* (l. 21, 22; see p. 27).

3   First person singular, negative, of the auxiliary *have* is *ain't* (l. 4; see pp. 25–6).

4   Third person singular, negative, of the auxiliary *do* is *don't* (l. 45; see p. 28).

5   The use of *lay* for standard English *lie* (l. 1) is not restricted to any region, and Standard English speakers often seem to have to concentrate hard to produce the appropriate form.

6   Items like *and all* (meaning *as well*) (l. 12), *like* (throughout), *and that* (l. 32) are also not restricted to any particular region, and are best regarded simply as features of colloquial speech.

7   Exclamations like *how the dickens* (l. 4) and *blimey* (l. 32) are colloquial, found in a number of regions of Britain, but are now used more by older people than younger ones.

8   *cos* (l. 29) represents /kɒz/, a colloquial form of *because*.

2 Norwich

2.1   The speech of Norwich in particular, and East Anglia in general, is southern.

(a) /ʊ/ and /ʌ/ are both present (WL 4, 5)

(b) /a/ and /ɑː/ are distributed as in RP (WL 21–6)

(c) the final vowel of *city*, etc., is /iː/ (WL 19, 20). Norwich English differs from the accents of London and the Home Counties (see p. 75) in that it lacks /l/ vocalization. Instead, [ɫ], with the back of the tongue raised towards the soft palate, is used (WL 27–31).

2.2   In Norfolk and neighbouring areas (see p. 67) /j/ is variably lost after all consonants (*humorous*, l. 1).

2.3   An older English distinction, lost in RP, is maintained. Thus words which are homophones in RP are quite distinct in Norwich:

/uː/	/əʊ/
moan	*mown*
sole	*soul*
nose	*knows* (WL 38, 39)

2.4   For some speakers, words like *moon* and *boot* have the same vowel (/uː/) as *moan* and *boat*, such pairs being homophonous (WL 11, 12).

2.5   The distinction between /ɪə/ and /ɛə/ found in traditional RP is not present, and so, for example, both *beer* and *bear* are pronounced /bɛː/ (WL 14, 15; *hear*, l. 19, 20; *here*, l. 16).

Map 5.2

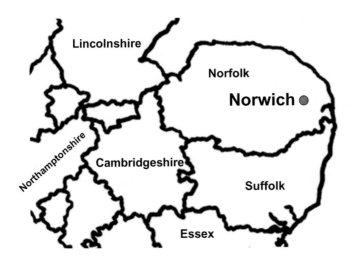

2.6   While /h/ has been preserved in rural East Anglia, it has been partly lost in Norwich. Thus in the recording it is generally present in stressed words, e.g. *humorous* (l. 1) and *husband* (l. 22), but is sometimes missing in unstressed words. Note (l. 26–7) that, within a second, *he* is produced first with /h/ and then without.

2.7   Certain words which have /əʊ/ in RP may have /ʊ/, e.g. *home* (l. 27) and *suppose* (l. 40).

2.8   Words like *room* and *broom*, and (as in other eastern accents – see p. 60) *roof* and *hoof*, have /ʊ/ rather than /uː/.

2.9   Stressed vowels are long, while unstressed vowels are much reduced, giving a distinctive rhythm to East Anglian speech. Associated with the reduction of unstressed vowels is the loss of consonants e.g. the loss of /v/ in *side of it* (l. 15).

2.10 *off* is /ɔːf/ (l. 23).

2.11 The glottal stop [ʔ] variably represents /t/ between vowels, and also accompanies /p, t, k/, particularly between vowels, e.g. *bottom* (l. 18), *dirty* (l. 23), *city* (WL 19).

2.12 *–ing* is /ən/.

2.13 The speaker uses [ʊ] in *right* (l. 11, 40), though for her this is clearly a sporadic feature.

The recording

The speaker is a woman about fifty years old who has lived in Norwich all her life. Her accent is quite strong. She recalls how she first met her husband.

The reader of the word list is a younger woman whose accent is less marked than the other Norwich speaker.

I've got something humorous happened to me, one thing I'll never forget. We ... well the ... this is the ... this is when I first met my husband ... cos I generally ... you know, my daughter always laugh about that. We went and had a drink, erm, one night. I don't know if
5 you know the Blue Room near the, erm ... Well, we went in there one night to have a drink. There was, erm, two girl friends and me – this was before I'd married, see – and, well this was the night, see, when I met my husband. And, erm, you know, they was like buy ... the fellows was buying us drinks and that, see, and, er, my friend and her
10 sister, oh, she say, well we don't want to go with them, she said, let's give them the slip. Right. Well we ran up, er, Prince of Wales Road, and opposite the ... well, that's ... that was the Regent then, that's the ABC now. There's a fruiterers, Empire Fruit Stores, I don't know if it's still there, is it? Well, there was this here fruits ... er, fruitstore and
15 that, and they had a passageway at the side of it, see. Well, my friends said to me, oh, they said, Flo, we'll get in here and give them the slip. I went to go in first, thought that was a long passage and that wasn't. They had forty steps and I fell right to the bottom. Yeah. And there was me, see, and we ... and we could hear ... you know, they could
20 hear these here fellows come run ... running up behind, see, so my friends said, oh quick, Flo have fell down a lot of stairs. Well, the one what's my husband, he said, let her lay there, he said. We've been treating you all night, they said, and you do us the dirty and run off! And they let me lay there. Well, any rate my friends, they managed to
25 stumble up. I had two big bumps on my head, I had a black eye, and course, erm, the ... erm ... see, my husband-to-be then, he ... well, he let me lay there. Well, when I got home, see, my father said to me, the first thing, whatever you done? I said I got knocked down by a bike. That was the first thing that come into my head. Yeah. And I ...
30 I gen ... generally tell my daughter about that. I said ... she say that's what you get, Mum, she say, for making a fellow, she said, letting a fellow, she said, buy you the drink and then, she said, run away from. I say yeah, but that, you know, that's sort of like, er ... well then he come round the next night to see how I was, and that's how we got
35 acquainted. He said, that'll teach you. He said that'll teach you, he say, er ... taking drinks off anyone, he said and try, he said, you thought, he said, you were going to slip off, he said, erm ... he said, did you know there was any steps? And I said, no I didn't. I thought that was a long passage, see, and there was just, there was forty steps
40 that go right down, I suppose, to ... and lead into a door at the back of this here fruit shop.

Notes

1 The third person singular, present tense is not marked by -*s*. Thus: *laugh* (l. 3), *say* (l. 10, 30, 31; see p. 28).

2 The absence of -*s* applies also to auxiliary *have* (l. 21).

3 Introduction of a relative clause by *what* (l. 22; see p. 29).

4 *lay* (l. 22): Standard English *lie* (as in the London recording).

5 *that* is used where standard English would have *it* (l. 17).

6 Note intrusive /ɹ/ in *by a bike* [bəɹəˈbɑɪʔk] (l. 28–9; see p. 64).

3 Bristol

3.1 The speech of Bristol, and the south-west generally, makes a distinction between pairs like *put* and *putt* (WL 4, 5). The vowel of *putt*, however, is [ə], and it seems that, unlike in RP, there are not two distinct phonemes /ə/ and /ʌ/ (see p. 60).

3.2 There is no /a/~/ɑː/ contrast (WL 21–26). /a/ is realized as [a] (Figure 5.2 and Map 4.1).

3.3 There is post-vocalic /ɹ/ (see p. 45 and Map 4.2). /ɹ/ is quite retroflex in quality (see p. 65): that is, it is articulated with the tip of the tongue bending backwards towards the hard palate (WL 14–18, 34–7, 42–4; note contrast with 45) and may justifiably be symbolized [ɻ]. Note that since this accent is rhotic, the equivalents of the RP diphthongs /ɪə/, /ɛə/, and /ʊə/ are /ɪɹ/ (WL 14), /ɛɹ/ (WL 15), and /ʊɹ/ (WL 42). See also section 3.13, below.

3.4 A feature of speech known as 'Bristol /l/', which is confined to the immediate area of Bristol, is the presence of /l/ following word

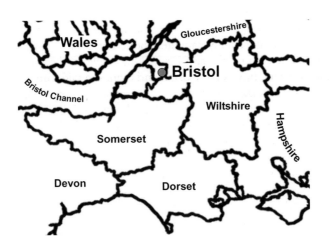

Map 5.3

final /ə/. Thus *America* may be /ə'mɛrɪkəl/ and *Eva* /'iːvəl/. In such cases *Eva* and *evil* are homophones. Bristol /l/ is not very common, however, is generally stigmatized, and cannot be heard on our recording (see p. 65). Note that although this 'intrusive' /l/ is an unusual phenomenon, it is not unique to Bristol: Gick (2002) reports a similar feature in the English of southern Pennsylvania.

3.5   Notice that dark /ɫ/ (see p. 45) is very dark: that is, the raising of the back of the tongue towards the soft palate is very marked.

3.6   There is a tendency in Bristol, though it is probably less common than in London, for the contrast between /θ/ and /f/ to be lost. Again, however, there is no example of this in our recording.

3.7   The glottal stop [ʔ] may represent [t] before a pause e.g. *Pete*, [pʰiːʔ] (l. 16), but note that in l. 11, *Pete* is [pʰiːt]).

3.8   The diphthongs /eɪ/ and /əʊ/ are rather wide, at [ɛɪ] and [ɔu] (Figure 5.2 and WL 8, 40, 41, and 29, 38, 39).

3.9   *–ing* is /ɪn/.

3.10 As in London speech, in words like *anything, something, –ing* may be /ɪŋk/ (l. 3, *something*).

3.11 (a) By comparison with RP, short vowels are often of longer duration. Thus: *job* [dʒɑˑb] (l. 26), *mad* [maˑd] (l. 11), and *bucket* ['bəˑkɪˑʔ] (l. 40).

(b) In certain words a 'fuller' vowel is used in an unstressed syllable than is the case for the equivalent in RP, e.g. /'gʊdnɛs/ (l. 26) as opposed to RP /'gʊdnəs/ or /'gʊdnɪs/.

(c) Similarly, a vowel followed by a consonant is found where in RP there is a syllabic consonant, e.g. ['bəʔən] as opposed to ['bʌtn̩] *button*.

Figure 5.2
Phonetic
qualities of
certain
Bristol
vowels

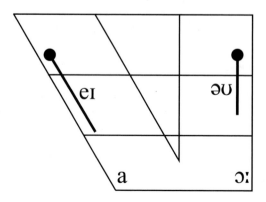

3.12 /h/ is variably absent. Thus in l. 3 it is present four times in succession (*He'd had his fixed, he said*), but is absent on the next occasion (l. 4), where *had* is [ad].

3.13 /ɪ/ is [ʊ] in *every* (l. 2).

The recording ———————————————————————

The speaker is a housewife, about thirty years old. Though she quite clearly comes from the Bristol area, her accent is less broad than most on the CD. As mentioned above, local features of pronunciation seem to become more frequent when she becomes excited.

You know our overflow ... well, a fortnight ago, next door neighbour said to us – mind, his overflows every day – ... could Pete do something about it. He'd had his fixed, he said. So Pete came in and went up and had a look. It's ... it's the ... erm ... you know, the
5 immersion heater system. I think it's where the ball thing doesn't close up properly, so the water drips out the overflow. Pete came up and had a go at it, and ever since then, two days apart from yesterday, is the only time ours has dripped out at all. Every day of the week theirs has dripped out. So yesterday afternoon Pete comes
10 home from fishing. I'm sure he waited for Pete, because he knows Pete won't say anything, see, cos I was mad. And, er, Pete comes in, and I heard all these doors going, and I went out and the hot water tap was on. So I said who's turned the hot water tap on? Pete said, he's just asked me again, can I do something about our
15 overflow. So I said well, you did tell him that his hasn't stopped since, he said. No, says Pete. And this morning I come down, and blow me if this isn't ... isn't overflowing again, this one. I mean, would you have the cheek to tell a neighbour to mend something when your own wasn't fixed? Well, it's our water that's making his wall damp. Not his
20 own water, mind, that flows out every day of the week. Just mine that's done three times in a fortnight. **[Comment from companion]** Oh, no, that was the guttering. Us, thinking we were being good, cleaned ours out regularly, but all we really did, see, it built up, the water then stayed in ours because it didn't go over the top of the dirt.
25 That is fixed ... that's been perfectly all right, even with the heavy weather, thank goodness. Point is, really, it's quite a simple job to fix it. Pete's Dad said really all you need is a new washer. Well, if he can just take the arm off, replace the washer and put it back, that's good, but if anything goes wrong I've then got to let the fire out, because I can't
30 have the fire going if the water can't be replaced. And so what is really a simple job, knowing us, could take all day. So I'd rather it dripped out there a bit longer. He reckoned he had somebody in, but, I mean,

if I had somebody in I would expect the job done properly. I mean, fair enough, Pete's just bent our arm. Well, he said it's the new
35 washer, but course it was doing a new washer down at the church that Pete's dad chopped all his hand the other week and had to have a week off work. And it's thinking of things like that that can happen to people who don't usually have calamities that makes me a bit worried about letting Pete do ours. It was this morning ... I went out this
40 morning to fill my coal bucket, it wa ... well, I don't ... I don't feel I should complain, because mine does drip out now and then, but knowing his does it every day ... I mean, it's a bit off isn't it, Jill?

Notes

1   Notice the infrequency of fillers like *kind of* and *like*.
2   *drips out the overflow* (l. 6) cf. Standard English, *out of the overflow* (see p. 32).
3   *course* (l. 35) = *of course*.

4 South Wales (Pontypridd)

4.1   In South Wales the distribution of /a/ and /ɑː/ is generally as in the north of England (see p. 60 and Map 4.1). The contrast between the vowels, however, is usually one of length only. Thus *cat* [kʰat] and *cart* [kʰaːt] (WL 21, 26).

4.2   (a) There is no post-vocalic /ɹ/, except in the speech of some native speakers of Welsh (Map 4.2).

(b) /ɹ/ is normally an alveolar tap [r] (see pp. 45, 65). That is, the tip of the tongue makes a rapid tap against the alveolar ridge (e.g. *tramline, right*, l. 2).

4.3   As in Bristol, there is no /ʌ/~/ə/ contrast. Words like *putt* (WL 5) have /ə/, contrasting with /ʊ/ in *put* (WL 4).

4.4   Words like *city* and *seedy* have /iː/ as the final vowel (WL 19, 20).

4.5   /l/ is clear in all environments (WL 27–31).

4.6   In words like *tune, few* and *used*, we find the diphthong /ɪu/ rather than /juː/ (*used*, l. 1). This diphthong is preserved even after /ɹ/ and /l/. Most speakers therefore make a distinction between pairs such as *blew* /blɪu/ and *blue* /bluː/ or *threw* and *through*. *Blew* and *blue* are contrasted in the short exchange at the end of the word list (see p. 67 and Figure 5.3).

4.7   Between vowels – when the first vowel is stressed – consonants may be doubled. So *city* (WL 19) is ['sɪtːiː].

4.8   /h/ is usually absent, but may be present in stressed positions e.g. *him*, l. 25.

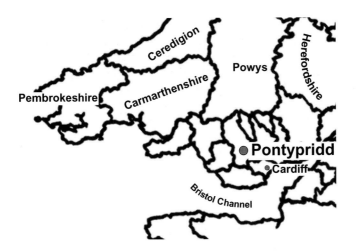

Map 5.4

4.9   (a) /eɪ/ is narrow, and may be a monophthong [eː] (Figure 5.3; WL 8, 40, 41).

(b) In certain areas of Wales a distinction is made between pairs of words like *daze* /deɪz/ and *days* /dɛɪz/. /ɛɪ/ occurs where there is <i> or <y> in the spelling. The speakers on the CD do not make this distinction.

4.10   /əʊ/ is narrow, and may be a monophthong [oː] (WL 12, 29, 38, 39). This tendency may result in such pairs as *so* and *soar* being homophones.

4.11   The vowel /ɜː/, as in *bird* (WL 16), is produced with the lips rounded, approaching [øː] in quality.

4.12   Intonation in Welsh English is very much influenced by the Welsh language. Though quite noticeable in the recording, it is less striking than in the speech of many Welsh people, including those whose first language is English. Welsh, which is spoken to a greater or lesser degree by around one-third of the population of Wales, is learned as a first language normally only in the west and north-west of the country. See further Walters (2001, 2003).

The recording

The speaker is a young man from Pontypridd, whose accent, though quite obviously Welsh, is not particularly marked. He is talking about an accident that happened to someone as a child.

The word-list reader is a young woman from Neath, near Swansea. Again, although she is clearly Welsh, her accent is not very strong.

Figure 5.3
Phonetic
qualities of
certain
South Wales
vowels

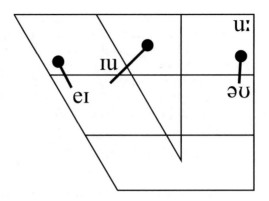

At the end of the word list there is the following exchange to demonstrate the difference between *blew* and *blue*:

Q: *What did the wind do yesterday?*

A: *Erm . . . the wind blew* /blɪu/ *strongly.*

Q: *All right . . . and what colour are your jeans?*

A: *My jeans are blue* /bluː/.

The tramline . . . ah, they used to have, erm . . . from the pit there used to be a tramline right to the top of the mountain . . . used to work on a, a pulley sort of system, I should think. I was too young to know then. They used to have about fifteen to twenty big pit drams on this
5   wire rope, and I would say it must have stretched, bottom to top, about three and a half, maybe four miles, and of course we'd winch up on it, pulled up, cos all the kids would be running up, jumping on it. And, er, I would say, well, there was one boy, how old is Gerin? Must be about thirty-eight. He's . . . jumped on and he fell off and it
10   cut his leg clean off. But they're big metal drams, they weighed . . . well, they must weigh about a ton with nothing in them. So you can imagine when they're full. And of course when they come down the journey again, they're coming down at a fair speed, cos they let them go down quite a bit and then they got the . . . an automatic brake, I
15   think, it slows them down. And they used to come down there. We used to jump on them on the top, and ride down. Things you do when you're young . . .

[asked how old the injured boy was at the time of the accident]

About ten, twelve. See, he won't . . . he's got a false leg but he won't wear it. When he wears it, you know, he . . . When he first had it he
20   used to wear it. And, er, he was qu . . . quite a big boy, as all Welshmen are, they're all broad. But he must be up to something like

twenty-eight stone, and he's really fat. It just hangs off him. He sits and watches television, and he has two pound of apples and, er, say a pound of chocolate. His mother makes sandwiches, she makes a loaf
25 of bread, you know, just for him, for sandwiches, as a snack. Well, most of the boys who drink with him in the club, erm . . . were with Gerin when he done it, when he done it. They used to . . . all used to ride up on the . . . the journey up. I should think every boy in Cil has done it.

[asked if he himself had ridden on the drams]

30 Oh, aye, regular. You'd always be warned – don't ride on the drams. Yeah, all right. Straight down the bottom and wait for them to come up, and you'd . . . you'd run up alongside them and just jump on. The most dangerous thing about that was, er, with the rope, the metal rope, which was about two inches in diameter, and it used to whip.
35 And of course you imagine a steel rope whipping. You . . . well, it'd cut a man clean in half. Well, you never see the dangers when you're young, do you?

Notes
1 *Two pound of apples* (l. 23): see p. 32.
2 *Done* as past tense of **do** (l. 27): see p. 27.
3 *Aye = yes* (l. 30): common in the north of England, Scotland, Ireland and Wales.

5 West Midlands

This is the accent spoken in Birmingham, Wolverhampton, and a number of other towns in that area (see Map 5.5).

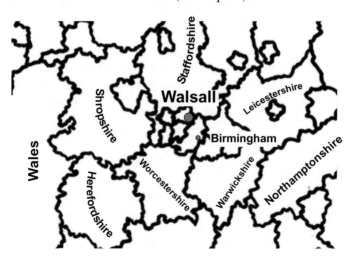

Map 5.5

5.1 The accent of the West Midlands is northern in that:

(a) /a/ is found in words such as *dance*, *daft*, etc. (see p. 60; WL 21–6)

(b) Pairs of words like *put* and *putt* are not distinct, /ʊ/ being the vowel in both (see p. 59; WL 4, 5).

5.2 The accent nevertheless has certain southern characteristics:

(a) The final vowel of *city* and *seedy*, etc., is /iː/ (see p. 62; WL 19, 20; cf. Liverpool), although the vowel in West Midlands accents is frequently realized as a diphthong which may be as wide as [ɜi] (see below).

(b) The diphthongs /eɪ/ and /əʊ/ are wide, being realized as [æɪ] and [ʌʊ] (Figure 5.4; WL 8, 40, 41 and 12, 29, 38, 39).

5.3 /iː/ is [ɜi] (Figure 5.4; WL 14, 19, 20).

/uː/ is [ɜu] (Figure 5.4; WL 28).

5.4 /aɪ/ is [ɔi] (Figure 5.4; WL 9, 46, 47).

5.5 /ɪ/ is very close, at [i] (Figure 5.4; WL 1, 19).

5.6 /ɜː/ and /ɛə/ are **merged** as [œː], e.g. *bear* (WL 15) and *bird* (WL 16). The influence of RP is, however, discernible in the attempted distinction on the word list between *fur* (WL 36) and *fair* (WL 27). This merger is not found throughout the West Midlands.

5.7 /h/ is usually absent.

5.8 *–ing* is /ɪn/.

5.9 Note that *one* is /wɒn/ but *won* is /wʊn/ (l. 25; see p. 60).

5.10 Glottal stop is infrequent in the speech of older speakers such as the Walsall man on the CD, but is now extremely common in that of young speakers (Mathisen 1999).

Figure 5.4
Phonetic qualities of certain West Midlands vowels

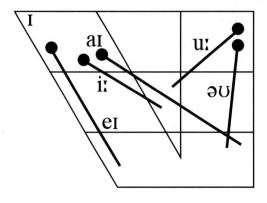

The recording

The speaker, a caretaker, is from Walsall and has a very distinctive West Midlands accent. After saying something about his evening habits, he goes on to talk about his footballing days, and then about the problems of Walsall Football Club.

I don't go out much, not in the week, you know. I go out one night a week, and if the wife isn't bothered, I won't, you know, I don't bother. Well, the wife and the daughter generally go out together and I'll stop in, you know, with the lad. But, er, as g . . . the wife and the daughter
5 they've booked up a show what the women have got up or summat, eight fifty to see that man who works . . . impersonates a woman. What's his name? Him who impersonates the women on the television?

The other night I couldn't get in . . . interested in it about ho . . .
10 homosexuals, you know. And I said to my wife, I says, er, you coming to bed? Her says, no, I'm going to see the finish of this. I says, all right then, goodnight, and I went up to bed. I mean . . . I'm not, you know, like that.

I used to be keen. I used to be a good footballer myself. Yeah.
15 Goodyears and all those, you know, they was high class teams. I mean you played for the honour then, I mean, you didn't get nothing out of it.

No, no, well, er, me and the captain of Guest Keens, we had a trial for Walsall and, er, we came up the one week, and they says come the
20 next week and play again, see. Well, in the meantime we'd got an important match for the works team, cup final, and the captain says, 'Are you going to Walsall?' I said, 'No, the works team's more important to me,' see. Course we didn't go, and we had a nasty postcard off Walsall FC about it, cos we didn't turn up.

25 Well, I won the one cup for them, really, in, erm, 1948. Er, we was, er, winning one-none half time, and the second half I got three goals, and we won four . . . a . . . an they s . . . and they made me go and have the cup, cos they said, 'You've won this cup and you're going to have it,' and I . . . I . . . was present . . . presented with it, you know.

30 I could have done, yes, if I'd have stuck to it, you know, but, er, well, when, you know . . . No, no . . . but I mean, you didn't get a lot then if you played professional. I mean, it was a poor wage then, years ago. But it . . . it was an honour to play. They didn't play for the money like they do today. Well, they've got to make it while they're fit, cos
35 you never know what's going to happen.

Well, Dave Mackay was on the wireless this morning before I come out, you know, and they was interviewing him, the reporter, and he said he . . . he couldn't understand it why they couldn't score at home, I mean, but win away, you know. Played for Derby, halfback, didn't
40 he? Yes, I do. I always like to see them win, and that, but, er . . . summat's lacking there, definitely.

Well, Walsall can if they dish the football up. Course they couldn't keep me away years ago. I used to go to every . . . well, I would think it's been about six or eight years, when they played Sunderland down
45 here in the cup, and Liverpool. I paid a man to do my job here of a Saturday afternoon to go and see the two matches. And when I come back – I was away, say, two hours – I'd still got the same work to do. Nothing had been done.

Well, er, they never spent no money, but they got local talent. They
50 got a lot of local talent what come up, you know, like, out of the amateur sides. That's where they go wrong, they don't go to the proper matches, er, like Shrewsbury. Now, Chick Bates, they had him from Stourbridge for about two hundred and fifty pound fee. He's scoring two or three goals a match now. I mean, Walsall could've
55 done with a man like him.

Notes

1   There are examples of multiple negation (see p. 24):
    You didn't get nothing out of it (l. 16–17).
    Well they never spent no money (l. 49).
2   Past tense of **come** is *come* (l. 36, 46, 50).
3   *I says* (l. 10) is 'historic present' (see p. 29).
    was is the past tense form of **be**, not only for the third person singular:
    We was winning (l. 25–6)
    they was interviewing him (l. 37).
4   *What* introduces a relative clause (see p. 29):
    they got a lot of local talent what come up (l. 49–50).
5   *summat* (l. 5) = Standard English *something*.
6   *not bothered* (l. 2) = not keen.
    the lad (l. 4), i.e. his son (cf. *the wife*).
    FC (l. 24) = Football Club.
    wireless (l. 36), meaning *radio*, is not regional but old-fashioned. It bears the same relationship to *radio* as *gramophone* does to *record player* (see p. 13).
7   *postcard off Walsall FC* (l. 24) = Standard English: *postcard from Walsall FC* (see p. 32).
8   *you* is /jaʊ/.
9   Dave Mackay (l. 36) is a former Scottish international footballer, and was manager of Walsall FC at time of recording.

10 *her* (l. 11) = *she*.

11 The definite article before a vowel is /ð/ e.g. *the amateur* (l. 50–1).

6 Leicester

Leicester is geographically very close to Walsall – the two cities are only 50 miles (80km) apart – but the dialects fall into the East Midlands and West Midlands groups respectively (see Map 4.3 on p. 70).

Map 5.6

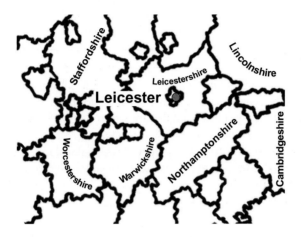

6.1 The accent of Leicester is northern in that:

  (a) Words like *dance* and *daft* have /a/ (WL 22, 23; see p. 60).

  (b) There is no distinction between pairs of words like *put* and *putt*: both have /ʊ/ (WL 4, 5; see p. 59).

6.2 Traditionally, the accents of the East Midlands area pattern with the southern English accents, in that the final vowel in words like *city* and *seedy* is /ɪ/ rather than /iː/. The speaker on the CD, however, is typical of young people in southern England who now generally have /iː/ in these words (WL 19, 20; see p. 62). /j/-dropping in words like *few* is also a traditional feature of East Midlands accents, though it cannot be heard in the CD recordings.

6.3 /eɪ/ and /əʊ/ are somewhat wider diphthongs than is the case in RP: [ɛ̝i] and [əʉ] are typical values.

6.4 The vowels /ɑː/ and the first element of /aɪ/ are quite back and often somewhat rounded at [ɑ̹ː] and [ɑi] or [ɒi], as in *bard* (WL 17), *tide* and *tied* (WL 46, 47).

6.5 In words like *cases* (l. 10), the second vowel is [ə] rather than the [ɪ] that is found in RP and many other accents.

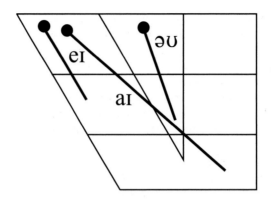

Figure 5.5
Phonetic
qualities of
certain
Leicester
vowels

6.6   As is increasingly the case for young people all over the British
      Isles, the speaker can be heard to use [ʔ] for /t/ in all phonological
      contexts (see p. 66). Examples are *airport* (l. 3), *what hour* (l. 3–4)
      out about (l. 4), *city* (l. 8), *bottle* (l. 17), etc.

6.7   Glottalization (p. 42) of final /p, t, k/ in final position is variable:
      compare *pit* and *pat* (WL 1, 3) with *pet* and *bout* (WL 3, 13; see
      p. 67).

6.8   The labio-dental [ʋ] can be heard occasionally, e.g. in *train* (l. 21),
      drinking (l. 26). See p. 5.

6.9   /l/ is frequently vocalized by this speaker, e.g. *pills* (l. 17)

6.10 *–ing* is very frequently /ɪn/, as in *tiring* (l. 2), *lugging* (l. 12).

6.11 The speaker uses [ɾ] for /t/ in intervocalic position, e.g. *at about*
      [ɾ] (l. 43). This feature, known as the **T-to-R rule** (Wells 1982:
      370), is found in other parts of the north of England, in Scotland
      and in Ireland. The Liverpool speaker (section 8) can also be
      heard to use it.

The recording

The speaker is a young man in his twenties from Ashby-de-la-Zouch, a
market town in north-west Leicestershire approximately 20 miles (32km)
from the city of Leicester itself, but the differences between Ashby and
Leicester in terms of accent are minor, particularly for someone of the
speaker's age.

[when asked about a favourite holiday]

You know, I went to Ireland for Ross's wedding. It was like . . . it was
a bit tiring, but we like went there . . . yeah, we got there on the
Thursday cos your dad took us to the airport, like, God knows what

hour of the morning. Well, we ended up flying out about eight o'clock
5 I think. We got into Dublin for nine. By the time we got through the
airport and everything else, cos we . . . like we got through the airport
and we got the bus from the airport to the bus . . . to . . . to the train
station in the city centre. By the time we got there we were waiting
round . . . we'd just missed the, like . . . the first train to where we were
10 going. And we had, like, loads of cases, so we couldn't be bothered to
sort of go out and take a walk round the city and that, cos we just
thought, well, to be honest, I don't really fancy lugging my case all the
way round. So we ended up . . . just sat in this pub in the train station
for about two hours. We had summat to eat, and then got on the train,
15 and I just passed out. That was it, good night. Cos it was about eleven
o'clock, and I was on the train just going like . . . I felt like I'd had a . . .
a bottle of sleeping pills or . . . When we got there, it was ridiculous,
cos everyone was trying to phone me, and my phone was just going
through to its answerphone. And so then, oh my God they've missed
20 the train. God, everyone thought . . . everyone was like going, where
you been, where you been? On the train. It was a good holiday
though. We just got . . . well, got leathered Thursday night, we took a
hundred and fifty quid with us each, and then I had my credit card
and Alex had her credit card, so like trains and, like, just . . . er, hotels,
25 and all of that like . . . we paid just under ten euros for a drink, well,
for a round. The Friday was even worse, the day of the wedding. We
got . . . started drinking at twelve, had a few drinks, went to the
church, ceremony rah rah rah rah rah, went back to the hotel . . . cos
we . . . me and Alex stayed in like the B and . . . like a B and B down
30 the road, which was actually a bit of a mistake, to be honest, because
we were sort of like quite out of the way. Taxi there, taxi back. And
when we came back it was like . . . we just went into the bar, and it was
drink drink drink, went in . . . and we were . . . it was quite fortunate,
because you sort of had free . . . you . . . you got a few drinks free
35 during the meal and that, but between twelve o'clock when we
started, and when we finished about five next morning, it was, like,
we'd clocked up . . . we must have spent about . . . between us
probably about two hundred quid or something. I looked at my wallet
the next day. I was like, 'I should close that and leave it well alone.'
40 We got back about . . . we must have got back about half-five in
the morning, or something. Then we had to get . . . then we got a
lift back to Dublin, because we thought . . . instead of staying down
there, cos . . . the trai . . . the train the next day was at about seven in
the morning, and to get to the train station and everything else, we
45 would have missed . . . we would have missed the flight, basically,
because there wasn't a train early enough to get back, you know. So
we go . . . we got a lift back to Dublin the next day, well, on the

Saturday, even, and we stayed in a hotel, and that was, like, that was nice.

Notes

1   *leathered* (l. 22) is a slang term meaning *drunk*, and is not confined to Leicester.
2   *summat* (l. 14) is /ˈsʊmət/ (cf. West Midlands, section 5).
3   The speaker makes frequent use of *like* as a pause filler, focus marker, and quotative (p. 23).
4   [mi] (l. 12) = *my*.
5   *Rah rah rah rah rah* (l. 28) is being used to indicate that the language used during the wedding ceremony was of a predictable, formalized nature and that the speaker had not really listened to what was being said.

7 Bradford

7.1   The accent of Bradford, and of Yorkshire generally, is northern in that:

(a) Words like *dance* and *daft* have /a/ (WL 22, 23; see p. 60). For some Yorkshire speakers, /a/ and /ɑː/ are differentiated only by length. For them the vowels are [a] and [aː] so *Pam* and *palm* are [pʰam] and [pʰaːm]. This, however, is not the case for the speakers on the CD, whose /ɑː/ vowels are a little further back.

(b) There is no distinction between pairs of words like *put* and *putt*: both have /ʊ/ (WL 4, 5; see p. 59).

(c) The final vowel in words like *city* and *seedy* is /ɪ/ (WL 19, 20; see p. 62).

Map 5.7

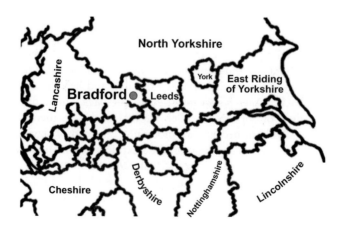

7.2 (a) /eɪ/ is either a narrow diphthong, or a monophthong [eː] (e.g. *plate*, WL 40; *mate*, WL 52; Figure 5.6). For some speakers, however, words which have <*eigh*> in the spelling (e.g. *weight*, WL 41) have /ɛɪ/.

(b) /əʊ/ is also either a narrow diphthong, or a monophthong [oː] (e.g. *boat*, WL 12; *nose*, WL 38; Figure 5.6), although for some speakers, many words which have <*ow*> or <*ou*> in the spelling (e.g. *knows*, WL 39) have /ɔu/. For these speakers *nose* and *knows* are not homophonous. This distinction (also made in Norwich – see p. 78) is being lost, as younger speakers generally use /əʊ/ for both sets of words (see further Watt and Tillotson 2001).

7.3 Pairs of words like *pore* (which has <*r*> in the spelling) and *paw* (WL 44, 45) are distinguished. Words without <*r*> have /ɔː/ ([ǫ̝ː]), while words with <*r*> have /ɔə/ ([ǫə]) (Figure 5.6). This distinction is also made by some RP speakers, though it is now rare.

7.4 (a) /ɛ/ is [ɛ̞], i.e. it is more open than in southern accents (WL 2).

(b) /uː/ is [uː] as compared with the more central realization of this vowel in Lancashire (WL 28).

(c) /aɪ/ is [aɛ] (WL 46; Figure 5.6).

7.5 In West Yorkshire (which includes Bradford) and other areas of Yorkshire, /b, d, g/ become /p, t, k/ when they immediately precede a voiceless consonant (i.e. a consonant produced without vibration of the vocal folds). The devoiced /d/ (effectively [t]) may then be realized as [ʔ], just as is common for /t/ in comparable positions in this accent. Thus *Bradford* is ['braʔfəd], and *could swing* (l. 22) is ['kʊʔswɪŋ].

7.6 /ɹ/ is a tap (see pp. 45, 65).

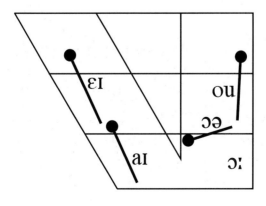

Figure 5.6
Phonetic qualities of certain Bradford vowels

7.7   /t/ in final position may also be realized as a glottal stop [ʔ] (e.g. *that*, l. 30; see p. 66).

7.8   *–ing* is /ɪn/.

7.9   /h/ is generally absent.

7.10   *make* and *take* are /mɛk/ and /tɛk/ (l. 38).

The recording

The speaker is a man who has lived in Bradford all his life. His accent is quite marked, but note the variable presence of /h/. He talks about his schooldays and events in his youth.

[asked if there were any schoolteachers he was afraid of or disliked]

Oh, aye, a Miss Ingham. Miss Ingham, when I was a kid, she . . . she always . . . to me she seemed rather vicious, you know, she'd knee you with her knee as she came round, you know, you were sat on the chair, and she'd kick her knee into your back if she thought, you know.
5   Priestley was . . . he was all right but . . . I . . . I think I was scared of him, really scared, you know, and when he came in – oh! – I couldn't think. 'Oh, he's coming in!' And honestly, I couldn't think when he were in sometimes, especially if he took us in mental arithmetic. Ooh, help. And when he took us in ear tests, that were as bad, nearly. He
10   used to . . . He'd tell you, he'd say sometimes, 'Put two fingers in your mouth!' you know, and have you putting two fingers in. 'Three!' 'Four!' 'Five!' 'Put your foot in!' Aye, you know, that sort of thing. He'd make you open your mouth that way. I mean, 'You couldn't sing with your teeth,' he said, 'like that, you know. Aye. You've got to open your
15   mouth to sing.' And he used to open his, and he'd about two teeth in the middle, sort of thing, what . . . All of us kids, you know, looked and he seemed to have three or four, you know, missing or more, happen, just two good . . . Oh aye, he were a lad, I tell you. As I say, he used to put such a fear into me I couldn't think. I remember that quite well.
20   Aye. Oh, wasn't I glad when he went out.

Well, one of the funniest when I . . . was playing on a swing bridge, you know, and, er, you were seeing how far you could swing the bridge out, and then, er t'swing bridge at Seven Arches. Swinging it out, you know, and you jump and see how far you can go on it. And
25   then one of them jumped into the canal, you see. He fell in. But that didn't finish, you see. We were . . . thought of making, er . . . dry his clothes. So they made a fire, took his clothes off, you see. And they couldn't get any slow-burning stuff, it were all quick-burning stuff,

you see. And then they were all running round with bracken and
30 things like that, making a big fire, and one kid ... holding his shirt,
you see, up to t'fire, and it caught fire. Burnt his shirt! Oh, the things
like that, you know, what you did as kids. Aye. We were caught red-
handed in this field, you know. 'What are you doing in here?' Well,
my brother just looked and says, 'What's up with you?' he says, 'this
35 is Farmer Budd's field.' We had no idea whether it were Farmer
Budd's one or not, you know, but this chap thought ... He were, er,
just, er, a chap that was keeping us out, you see, and ... You know,
our Clifford had just the presence of mind to say ... make out that he
knew the farmer, which we didn't.

Notes

1   Past tense of **be** is *were* (l. 8) for all persons.
2   *You were sat* (l. 3) = *You were sitting*. *I was sat*, *I was stood* are widely used in
    parts of the north and west of England, rather than *I was sitting*, *I was*
    standing.
3   *he'd about* (l. 15). This is the full verb **have** (see p. 21).
4   *the* may be [ʔ] (e.g. *to t'fire*, l. 31). This phenomenon is known as **definite**
    article reduction, and is extremely common in Yorkshire dialects, to the
    point that it is a very well-known and stereotyped feature of these varieties
    (see further Jones 2002).
5   *always* (l. 2) is /'ɔːləz/, a form found in other accents.
6   *kid* for *child* (l. 30) is colloquial and not restricted to any particular area.
7   *happen* (l. 17) = *perhaps*.

8 Liverpool

The accent of Liverpool is limited to the city itself, to urban areas
adjoining it, and to towns facing it across the River Mersey (although its
influence may be detected in other neighbouring accents, even as far
away as north Wales). While the accent is northern rather than southern
in character, it differs in a number of ways from other northern urban
varieties, including those of the rest of Lancashire, the county in which
Liverpool formerly stood. Some of the differences show the influence of
the large numbers of Irish people, especially from southern Ireland, who
have settled in Liverpool over the last two centuries.

8.1   The Liverpool accent is northern in that:

(a) There is no contrast between pairs of words like *put* and *putt*,
    both being /pʊt/ (WL 4, 5). There is no /ʌ/ vowel.

(b) /a/ occurs in words like *dance*, *daft*, etc., which in RP have /ɑː/
    (see p. 60; WL 21–6).

Map 5.8

(c) Words like *book* and *cook* have the vowel /uː/ (see p. 60; there are no examples on the CD).

8.2   Unlike in other northern urban accents (but in common with Newcastle), the final vowel of words like *city* and *seedy* is /iː/ (see p. 62).

8.3   There is no contrast in Liverpool speech between pairs of words like *fair* (RP /fɛə/ ~ /fɛː/) and *fir* (RP /fɜː/) (WL 34–7). The most typical realization of the vowel is [ɛː], but other forms, including [ɜː], are also heard.

8.4   (a) /p, t, k/ are heavily aspirated or even affricated (cf. London, p. 76). Thus:

   can't (l. 5) [kxɑːnt]

   straight (l. 11) [streɪts]

   back (l. 17) [bakx]

   In final position, /p, t, k/ may be realized as fricatives [ɸ, s, x].

(b) Related to this phenomenon is the relative infrequency of glottal stops in Liverpool speech.

(c) Between vowels, the first of which is short, /t/ may be realized as [ɾ] through application of the T-to-R rule (see p. 92). This is limited to certain lexical items, e.g. *matter, what, but, get* (e.g. l. 21, [gɒɾədʒɒb] *got a job*).

8.5   /ɹ/ is usually a tap, [ɾ] (see pp. 45, 65) (e.g. *three*, l. 1; *real*, l. 4; *cigarettes*, l. 6).

8.6   /h/ is usually absent, but is sometimes present (e.g. l. 40, *him and her*).

8.7   /eɪ/ and /əʊ/ are narrow diphthongs (WL 8, 40, 41 and WL 12, 38, 39) (Figure 5.7).

8.8   Initially, /ð/ may be [d] (e.g. l. 10, [dɛː] *there*).

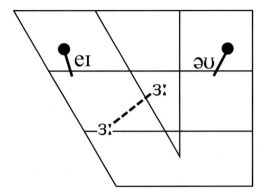

Figure 5.7
Phonetic qualities of certain Liverpool vowels

8.9 (a) The suffix *-ing* is /ɪn/.

   (b) Words like *singer* and *thing* (see p. 67) have [ŋg]. A clear example, because it precedes a vowel, is *thing*, l. 18.

8.10 All the features mentioned so far have covered particular segments of speech. But there is another feature, **velarization**, which is present throughout Liverpool speech and which gives it a distinctive quality. Velarization is the accompaniment of other articulations by the raising of the back of the tongue towards the soft palate, as in the production of dark [ɫ].

The recording

The speaker is a middle-aged barmaid who has lived all her life in Liverpool. She talks about pubs she knows, and people who work in them. The word-list reader is younger and has a less pronounced accent.

Yeah, she's gone to America for three weeks, so we all go sad . . . dead sad again next week. She comes over . . . I'll go polishing everything next week. She's a good manager, like, isn't she? But, er . . . she's a real Annie Walker, you know. Everything's got to be so. She's . . . once
5 you get to know her, she's great. But you can't drink, and you can't have a smoke. We're all walking round with four lighted cigarettes in our hand and having a drink off everyone that gives us one. Yeah, we're in charge, yeah. At least, he's, er, in charge of them all, and I'm the monitor. I'm, er . . . when he's not there, I'm in charge. But, er, it's
10 . . . I tell you what, if she left I wouldn't go out there. Cos, you know, I do really like working for her. She's straight, and she trusts you, and that's imp . . . that's the main thing, like, isn't it, you know? She is . . . she's great. I don't think she's ever laughed till I went there . . .

Cos as I say, when you do your work you don't need, erm, a boss, do
15 you? That's what I say. You know, this . . . this manager's made up.
He said, erm . . . he's never co . . . he'll give us the tills, then he comes
back about four o'clock, and we've all locked up and gone, everything
for him. He says, one thing about it, he says, 'I haven't got to stand
over youse.' Only the night time, you know. Course, where it is, on a
20 night they have a lot of, er, you know, some that'll come a couple of
nights, all these part-time students, and some of them, er . . . got a job,
and going to Spain, and . . . they'll want a few bob extra and then they
just leave it. I don't know whether they tap her till or what they do,
but . . . he . . . he has to be there for them of a night time. Yeah, but
25 it is, it's, er . . . and it's a pub that you wouldn't be frightened to
bring anybody into, isn't it? You know, it's beautiful . . . er, yeah. True,
yeah. Oh, well, you . . . you say . . . I say bye-bye in there, say ta-ra up
there.

Mind, she'll be round there drunk now if you went into the Winifred
30 for a drink. Th . . . I've never seen barmaids like them. They go round
well away, shouting and everything, and . . . and the boss and the
manageress are standing watching them. But they must be all right,
kind of thing, or otherwise they wouldn't put up with it, would they,
like? True, yeah. Yeah. Well, this is it. Mind you, there's been three
35 man . . . three managers, er, sacked from there for bad takings. So they
can't be, er, all that good. And two of them is . . . two that's been
through each . . . one that's, you know, er, been sacked. But then, after
that there was, erm, a stout one named Jean. And John. She was, er,
an Australian, I think. Yeah, and . . . She was here that long waiting for
40 a place that I took her in for three weeks. Him and her. And they were
. . . she was a great person. I was made up because I didn't take no
rent off her, Stan, cos I was . . . every halfpenny she had had gone
paying for storage of furniture, and she had dogs, and . . . all that, so I
just let her live here, like. But she used to have a caterer in there as
45 well, like Mrs Crighton. When I come home I'd have a three-course
dinner, and I couldn't leave a handkerchief down it was washed and
ironed. I was made up because I didn't have to do nowt to help her.
But, anyhow, he . . . he finished up, erm . . . er, a night watchman on
Runcorn Bridge. That's the only place she could get a house, was
50 Runcorn. It was a shame, like, with the money she had, and she was
in . . . born in New Zealand, and everything, and, er, staff pulled her
right down. It is. She said to me, she said, 'Bridie,' she said, 'they
didn't take it in handfuls, they took it in fistfuls.' And she was a really
good manager t . . . to them, you know. You know, especially
55 Christmas, she wouldn't buy them a box of handkerchiefs, or
something like that, be a suit. Or a dress. And buy all their children.

But yet they done all that on her like, you know. Yeah. Wouldn't be Mrs Crighton. She'd only l . . . find her once and that would be your lot, you're through the door.

Notes

1   There is multiple negation (see p. 24):
    I didn't take no rent off her (l. 41–2)
    I didn't have to do nowt to help her (l. 47)
2   Past tense of **come** = *come* (l. 45); past tense of **do** = *done* (l. 57; see p. 27).
3   *youse* (/juːz/ when stressed, and /jəz/ when not stressed) is the plural form of *you*. It is fairly common throughout non-standard varieties of British and Irish English.
4   The speaker makes a distinction between *bye-bye* and *ta-ra*, both meaning *goodbye* (l. 27). She uses the former in settings she regards as socially superior.
5   *Annie Walker* (l. 4) was a well-known character in the television soap opera *Coronation Street*. She was a pub landlady who was strict with her staff.
6   There are some perhaps unfamiliar lexical items:
    bob (l. 22) = a shilling (twelve pence) in pre-decimal currency. The term continued to be used after decimalization in 1971, and in fact the shilling piece was used for some years after this as the equivalent of five new pence.
    made up (l. 41) = very pleased.
    tap (l. 23) = take money from.
    well away (l. 31) = drunk.
    where it is (l. 19) = *the thing is*.
7   *like* (l. 3), *you know* (l. 4), *kind of thing* (l. 33), are common colloquialisms in all varieties of British and Irish English.

9 Edinburgh

The vowel systems of Scottish English accents are radically different from those of English in England, and it is therefore not especially helpful to describe them in terms of differences from RP. Scottish Standard English speakers (see p. 12) most usually have vowel systems approximately as given below (with words in which these vowels appear).

/i/	*bee beer*			/u/	*pull put*
	seedy meet				*boot poor*
	meat				
/e/	*bay plate*	/ɪ/	*pit bird*	/o/	*pole boat*
	weight		*fir city*		*board nose*
	their mate				*knows*

/ɛ/ *pet fern*   /ʌ/ *putt fur*   /ɔ/ *cot caught*
     there   *paws pause*
                                                    paw pot
                                                    Paul doll

                        /a/ *bard hat*
                             dance daft
                             half father
                             farther

/aɪ/ *buy*   /aʊ/ *bout*   /ɔɪ/ *boy*

Figure 5.8
Phonetic
qualities of
certain
Edinburgh
vowels

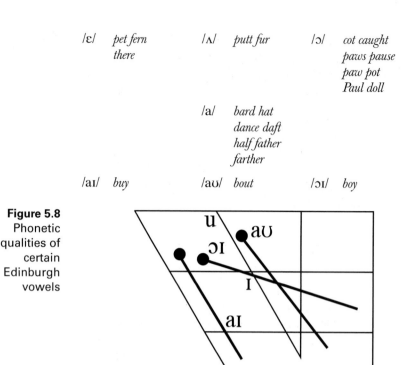

It will be noted that:

9.1   Vowels such as RP /ɪə/ and /ɜː/ do not occur (though see 9.3, below). This is because Scottish accents are rhotic – that is, they preserve post-vocalic /ɹ/ (see p. 63), the loss of which in English English led to the development of these newer vowels. Pairs of words like *bee* and *beer* (WL 7, 14) thus have the same vowel, but are distinguished by the presence or absence of /ɹ/. The /ɹ/ may be realized as a tap [ɾ] (see p. 45), an alveolar approximant [ɹ], a retroflex approximant [ɻ], and occasionally a trill [r], though the last of these is not as common in Scottish English as the stereotyped or 'stage' form of the accent would lead one to believe. There is evidence dating back several decades that rhoticity is being lost in some urban areas of Scotland, however (see Stuart-Smith 2003).

9.2   Pairs of words such as *cot~caught* (WL 32, 33), *pull~pool* (WL 27, 28), and *Pam~palm* are not distinguished (p. 62). Length is not generally a distinctive feature of Scottish vowels. Monophthongs tend to be 'pure', in the sense there is no trace of diphthongization, although for many middle- and upper-class speakers /e/ and /o/ may be markedly diphthongal, having values

Map 5.9

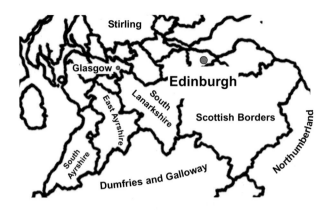

very similar to those found in RP. The word-list reader has [ei] in *bay*, *plate* and *weight* (WL 8, 40, 41) but [e] in *mate* (WL 52), and has [o] for /o/ throughout (WL 12, 29, 38, 39).

9.3   For many Scottish speakers, words such as *fern*, *fur* and *fir* have different vowels. Different accents differ as to how far they preserve this distinction (WL 34, 35, 36), and in urban areas of Scotland the trend appears to be one involving the collapse of these vowel qualities towards an RP-like [ɜː], though generally the post-vocalic /ɹ/ is retained (see 9.1, above).

9.4   A distinction is made between pairs of words like *tide~tied* (WL 46, 47) and *booze~boos*, the second vowel in each case being longer. The basis for the distinction is that the second word in each pair has a word-final vowel plus an inflectional ending: *tie + d* (cf. London *pause~paws*, p. 75). This alternation is the consequence of a complex vowel length conditioning system formerly known as **Aitken's Law**, and now more generally known as the **Scottish Vowel Length Rule** (see Scobbie, Hewlett and Turk 1999).

9.5   A distinction is made between pairs of words like *which* /ʍɪtʃ/ and *witch* /wɪtʃ/. /ʍ/ is effectively a voiceless [w] produced with audible friction at the lips, and is rather like the sound made when blowing out a candle.

9.6   Two accents – Edinburgh and Glasgow – are used here to exemplify the English of urban central Scotland. While there are considerable differences between Edinburgh speech and the speech of other Scottish cities (such as Aberdeen – see section 10) the accents of Edinburgh and Glasgow are sufficiently similar to act as a good guide as to what to expect in central Scotland in general. In listening to accents of Scottish English, the following points should also be noted.

(a) /ɪ/ tends to be central [ï] or [ə], and /u/ is markedly fronted at [ʉ] or even [y].

(b) [ʔ] is a frequent realization of /t/ (see pp. 42–3; *better*, l. 9; *that*, l. 11).

(c) /h/ is present.

(d) *–ing* is /ɪn/.

(e) While the accents of Edinburgh and Glasgow are broadly similar in terms of their segmental characteristics (i.e. the individual speech sounds used), they are markedly divergent in their intonation patterns. Edinburgh English is fairly similar to RP in terms of intonation, in that stressed syllables are signalled by a rise in pitch. Speakers from Glasgow, however, tend to mark stress on syllables using a fall in intonation (this is true also of Belfast English: see section 11, below).

The recording

There are two main speakers on the CD. The word-list reader is from Glasgow and was studying at an English university at the time of recording. Although her accent clearly identifies her as Scottish, it is by no means especially strong.

The second speaker is from Edinburgh, and his accent is rather stronger than that of the word-list reader (he has, for example, glottal stops representing /t/ between vowels). He talks about a certain area of Edinburgh as it was when he was young.

They were high tenement buildings and, er, many, er, sub-let houses, you know, broken up, er, bigger houses into . . . the room and kitchen was about the average house in these days, what we called the room and kitchen, with perhaps a toilet inside or outside on the landings,
5 but there was no such things as bathrooms in these days in these areas, you know?

Adam Street, which was in the centre of that area, there was some very very good houses, rather old-fashioned, but quite good houses with fairly big rooms and that, and these were sort of better-class
10 people, er, people with maybe . . . s . . . minor civil servants and things like that, you know, that had . . . be able to afford dearer rents and that in these days, you know? But the average working-class man, the wages were very small. The rents would run from anything from about five shillings to seven shillings, which was about all they could
15 have possibly afforded in these days. It didn't . . . it didn't re . . . matter how many a family you had, er, if it was two rooms, well, Devil take the hindmost! [laughter] Aye, and you couldn't get out of your

environment, you see, you just had to suffer it and make the b . . .
most of it. And they all survived, that was the great thing. [laughter]
20 No, I think they were better fed than these days, you know. The . . . at
least, the quality of the food was better, I think, and the meat . . . No,
that's correct . . . it was, er . . . pretty coarse meal, and all that sort of
thing, and everything was much more, er, farm produce was much
more naturally grown, and things like that. So that . . . very big
25 families, you know, the . . . the average family was n . . . nothing under
five children in a family . . . very, very rarely. Oh, you'd have them
anything up to nines. Nine in a family living in two rooms. There was
no segregation, or anything like that. The only hope was that
somebody would get married or something like that, you know. Th
30 . . . it was some great stories in that area, you know, it was some really
. . . people were . . . they were quite, er, amusing that the, er, how they
overcame their difficulties, you know. They could improvise, if . . . I
remember a very funny thing, though I don't . . . I was quite young at
the time, but there was a place in the Pleasance, off the Pleasance,
35 called Oakfield Court, and it was a very, very rough quarter.
Everybody fought with each other in . . . in circulation. Er, one fought
one one week or . . . It was just drink and a fight, you know, er, very
clean fighting, that, er, when they got into a good mood, they had
what they called a party called a 'surpriser'. And they . . . somebody
40 took the bed down in one of the houses and, er, moved the furniture
out into the street and all that, and they got two or three bottles of
beer and had a party, and, er, they were very lucky if it lasted to the
fight started again. [laughter]

Notes

1   *with* is consistently /wɪ/. In more prestigious Scottish speech, *with* is /wɪθ/
    rather than /wɪð/.

2   *this* and *these* with time reference may be found in Scottish English where *that*
    and *those* are used in standard English English (l. 3).

10 Aberdeen

The English of Aberdeen is still heavily influenced by the conservative
'Doric' dialect of Scots (see section 16, below) which is spoken
throughout the north-eastern part of Scotland. In Aberdeen city itself,
however, the accent used by many younger speakers approaches those of
the central belt cities of Edinburgh and Glasgow. As with Glasgow, the
English used in Aberdeen is probably best viewed as lying towards the
middle of a spectrum ranging from Scottish Standard English at one
extreme to broad Doric Scots at the other, with no clear demarcation
between the two (see McClure 2002).

Map 5.10

10.1 The accent is consistently and markedly rhotic. Variants of /ɹ/ used by the speakers on the CD include [ɾ], e.g. in *Torry* (l. 2), *brought* (l. 2), *three* (l. 2), *horrified* (l. 5); [ɻ], as in *top-floor* (l. 7), *cards* (l. 41), *beer* and *bear* (WL 14, 15), and the alveolar trill [r] in *bird* (WL 16), *fir* (WL 24), and *fur* (WL 36). Note that the word-list speaker devoices some of these. As mentioned above, trilled [r] is not quite as common in Scottish accents as many people believe: it is generally associated with emphatic pronunciations, and its frequency in the word list probably stems from the fact that the reader is speaking carefully.

10.2 There is uvularization of second /ɹ/ in *father* (WL 25). Wells (1982: 411) remarks that the use of uvular [ʁ] is surprisingly common as a 'personal idiosyncrasy' in north-eastern Scotland, but that it is not sufficiently common that we can regard it as a feature of north-eastern Scottish accents *per se*.

10.3 /l/-vocalization is common (e.g. *Paul*, WL 30).

10.4 [ʔ] is very common in casual speech among younger Aberdonians, e.g. *brought up* (l. 2), *better* (l. 12), *eight* (l. 14), *right* (l. 16). Glottalling of /p, t, k/ in intervocalic positions in words like *paper* and *butter* can sometimes be heard, giving pronunciations with qualities reminiscent of those found in Northumbrian English (see section 15, below).

10.5 There is comparatively little aspiration on word-initial /p, t, k/. Examples are heard in *top* (l. 7), *people* (l. 24), *cars* (l. 38), *pit* (WL 1), *pot* (WL 6). Presumably so as to ensure contrast between the voiceless stops and the voiced ones, /b, d, g/ are often pre-voiced (e.g. *bee, bay*, WL 7, 8; *doll* WL 31), as per French or Spanish.

10.6 A stereotypical feature of Aberdonian speech, and north-eastern Scottish English more generally, concerns the realization of /ʍ/ as [f] or [ɸ]. This, in combination with various differences in the vowel system, yields north-eastern Scots pronunciations such as

/fuː/ for *who*, /faɹ/ for *where*, and the characteristic /fɪt/ for *what*. Examples in the main recording are *when* (l. 46) and *what* (l. 58).

10.7 Vowels which have undergone merger to /ɜː/ in RP remain contrastive in the speech of older Aberdonians: compare the vowels of *fir* /fɪɹ/, *fern* /fɛɹn/ and *fur* /fʌɹ/ (WL 34, 35, 36); see Figure 5.9. These contrasts, as elsewhere in Scotland, are tending to collapse towards /ɜː/ in the speech of many younger Scots, however (see above).

10.8 /a/ is often very back: *after* (l. 2), *married* (l. 6), *flat* (l. 7), *wax* (l. 55); see Figure 5.9. The word-list reader – uncharacteristically for this accent – has [ɑ] in *dance*, *daft* and *half* (WL 22, 23, 24), though there is no other evidence that he might have a distinction between /a/ and /ɑː/ of the sort found in English English accents.

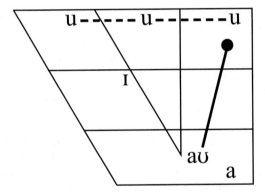

Figure 5.9 Phonetic qualities of certain Aberdeen vowels

10.9 /u/ is often much further back than in Edinburgh or Glasgow English: the [u] in *pool* (WL 28), *move* (l. 8), and *through* (l. 11) approaches a quality in the region of cardinal vowel 8. There are other cases in which the vowel has much fronter quality at [ʉ] or even [y], e.g. *two* (l. 26).

10.10 Both elements of the diphthong /aʊ/ are backer than in the accents of central Scotland (*now*, l. 6; *downhill*, l. 19).

10.11 *-ing* is often /ɪn/, e.g. *living* (l. 2), *cutting* (l. 10)

10.12 *that* very often lacks any initial consonant, so that the phrase *that's that* may be pronounced [atsat]. An example of this in the recording is in the phrase *like that* (l. 4).

10.13 *all* is [a] (e.g. l. 4).

10.14 *houses* is /haʊsɪz/ (l. 26).

The recording

The accent is represented by two speakers. The main speaker is a woman in her forties, while the word-list reader is a man of about the same age. Both have lived all their life in Aberdeen, or in towns close to the city.

Well, I was born in Footdee, which is across the River Dee from Torry, where I was brought up after I was three. And ... just living beside the seaside, really. Ideal childhood. Went to school there, things like that. We used to roam, climb the cliffs, all the things you
5 werena supposed to do, you would be horrified at your ain kids daeing now. Well, when I got married at nineteen, we did ha ... our very first flat was a top-floor tenement flat in Torry, again. We didna move very far. And, er, it was an old-fashioned flat, you know, the toilet was on the stairway between the two flats. And at that time they
10 were cutting back on all the grants that you could get to redevelop older properties, so when the grant fell through we decided we were better just to buy new. So we moved out to Ellon and we bought the last plot up in Ness Circle. And we're now on our third house in Ellon. We've been here for eight years now.

[asked how Aberdeen has changed in recent decades]

15 Well, like in the eighties when it was all oil office buildings and things, they were sort of throwing up skyscrapers left, right and centre, we ... and filling them with office space which ... half of that's vacant now. And a l ... as the oil kind of tailed off a bit the shops started to go downhill, but now it's sort of reviving itself and getting its act together.
20 But it's still sort of behind the times. There's nae ... not a lot of pedestrianized areas, or ... you know, other big cities you can go and roam about and it's easy ... easily accessible, where it's not really in our main s ... main street.

[asked how Footdee has changed since her childhood]

Oh yes, it's all very trendy now. Yes, it's all foreign people that live
25 there now. [laughter] Erm ... yeah, they were, erm, great thick walls, cottage-type houses, maybe two storeys at the most, mostly in rows for protection against the wind, really, more than anything. But still where ... near enough the sea that the waves would hit the roof in the winter. Scary.

[asked about life in rural Aberdeenshire in winter]

30 Aye, well, we were once coming back from Aberdeen in the winter when the winters were really bad, and you'd no sense of where the middle of the road is or anything. And before it was all dual

carriageway and everything it was quite a windy road. And I can
remember one winter struggling to get round this hill bend, and actually
35 discovering we were on the wrong side of the road when we we got to
the top of the bend. And we'd nowhere to go. You couldn't …
couldn't just pull over left, cos the snowdrifts were so bad. So, 1 …
like, both sets of cars are sliding sort of sideways together. We never
actually hit, but it was like slow motion, like, 'This is it!' a sort of…

[asked about leisure pursuits and her work as a childminder]

40 Leisure time, well, I do a lot of cross-stitch, and I like to make … I do
papercraft things, cards … I like doing that, it's nice and relaxing. I
know that Lisa's an age she can fit in with that, she quite likes all that
arty kind of things as well.

I always liked young children. Nae so keen on teenagers, but …
45 unfortunately mine are heading that way! But, erm, before I had my
own children, when you think you know all the … the theory of it,
once your own come along that goes right out the window. So I
decided no, I c … I could do this a lot better than retail, so…

When … well, Ross was six and Lisa would be nearly three, we were
50 selling the flat to buy this house here. So everything's spick and span
for this first viewing, and we would have an early tea because this
gentleman was coming at seven o'clock, and we wanted everything
tidied away, and … no smelly kitchens. So we were going great guns.
Kids were very quiet. I stuck my head in the living room door to find
55 wax crayon written all over an oatmeal-coloured carpet, and my two
sitting there with the wax crayons writing into the carpet. No paper in
sight. So I'm saying, 'Try and be calm. Right, how are we going to do
this?' 'What do you think you're doing? You've got every colour of
wax crayon on that carpet!' 'No,' says my son, and produces a white
60 crayon from behind his back, telling me the white crayon doesn't
work. But however, with a lot of scrubbing and an iron and a piece of
brown paper, with the children plunked on the top bunk-bed
meanwhile, we got it cleaned up before this chap would come. In the
end, after all that fuss, he didn't buy the flat. But never mind, we got
65 there in the end.

Notes

1   *ain* (l. 5) = *own*
2   *daeing* (l. 6) = *doing*
3   Note the speaker's use of *that* + plural noun phrase in *that arty kind of things*
(l. 42–43); see p. 34.

Map 5.11

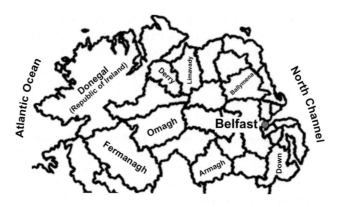

11 Belfast

In the northern part of Northern Ireland speech is quite similar to that of Scotland, which is where large numbers of settlers to Ulster came from. Many of these settlers would have spoken Scots, and a form of the language known as Ulster Scots is still spoken in the province today. In the south of the province, on the other hand, speech derived originally from that of the West Midlands and the south-west of England. Belfast speech combines features from both north and south.

11.1   As in Scotland, there is post-vocalic /ɹ/ (see p. 63). /ɹ/ is realized as a retroflex, frictionless approximant [ɻ] (see p. 65). It is similar to word-initial /ɹ/ in RP, except that the tip of the tongue is pulled back somewhat further.

11.2   (a) The vowel system is similar to that of Scottish accents:

/i/	*bee beer* *seedy meet* *meat*				/u/	*put boot* *pull pool* *poor*
/e/	*bay bear* *plate weight* *mate*	/ɪ/	*pit fir* *bird city* *fern fur*		/o/	*boat board* *pole knows* *nose pour* *pore*
/ɛ/	*pet*	/ʌ/	*putt*		/ɔː/	*Paul paw* *doll pause* *caught*
		/a/	*pat bard* *hat dance* *daft half* *father farther*		/ɒ/	*cot*
/aɪ/	*buy* *tide* *tied*	/aʊ/	*bout*		/ɔɪ/	*boy*

(b) Vowels are short before /p, t, k, tʃ/, and long before other consonants or when final (cf. the Scottish Vowel Length Rule, discussed on p. 103).

(c) In Belfast speech the actual realization of a vowel may vary considerably according to the sound which follows it. For example, /a/ in *daft* has a realization not very different from /ɑː/ in RP, while in *bag* it may be [ɛ] (Figure 5.10). Since the vowel in *beg* may also be [ɛ], the two words may not always be distinguished. This raises the question of whether it would be better to consider the vowel in *bag* to be /ɛ/ rather than /a/. For various reasons we have chosen not to do this, but the reader should be aware that the analysis of vowels could have been somewhat different from the one we propose (cf. /e/ vs. /ɛ/, and /o/ vs. /ɔː/).

11.3 The intonation of Belfast English, the speech of people from Northern Ireland generally, is (loosely) characterized by rising tones on statements, rather than falling ones, as is the case in RP. According to Rahilly (1997), this means that the typical pitch pattern of an utterance such as *It has changed out of all recognition now since our day*, in which we can identify two particularly strongly stressed syllables (the third syllable of *recognition* and *our*), will be one involving an abrupt lowering of pitch on these stressed syllables, followed on the next syllable by a sharp rise to a substantially higher pitch. This is much the same pattern as can be found in Glasgow English.

11.4 The following notes on vowels should be read in association with Figure 5.10:

(a) /u/ is central, [ʉ].

(b) /e/ is normally realized as a diphthong varying between [ɛə] and [iə], but in words like *bay* (WL 8) and *say* (l. 12) the vowel is a monophthong, [ɛː]. In plural and possessive forms of

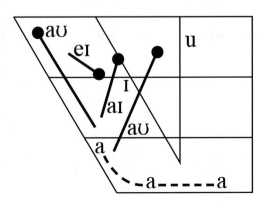

Figure 5.10
Phonetic
qualities of
certain
Belfast
vowels

these words, too, the vowel is [ɛː] (e.g. *days*, l. 40), and *days* therefore contrasts with *daze*.

(c) /ɪ/ is fairly central, [ɨ]. Although *fir, fur, fern* and *fair* may sometimes have different vowels, they all tend to be pronounced with [əɹ], which is probably best analysed as /ɪɹ/.

(d) /ɔː/ and /ɒ/ contrast only before /p, t, k/, as in *caught* and *cot* (WL 32, 33).

(e) As was mentioned above, realizations of /a/ may vary considerably. Before certain consonants (e.g. /f/ and /s/ in *daft*, WL 23, and *class*, l. 14) there is a back or central realization. Before other consonants the vowel is front, and before /g/ and /ŋ/ may be raised to [ɛ]. (There is no example on the CD with /g/ or /ŋ/, but *back*, l. 10, is [bæk].)

(f) /aɪ/ is variable, but is often [ɛɪ] (WL 9, 46, 47).

(g) /aʊ/ is very variable. Typical realizations are [æʉ] and [ɛi] (WL 13; *house*, l. 1; *down*, l. 5).

11.5 In some rural areas of the province, /j/ may be found after /k/ and /g/ before front vowels in words like *car*, [kjaɹ]. This phenomenon is now vestigial in Belfast, and there are no examples on the CD.

11.6 Between vowels /ð/ may be lost, so *mother* may be ['mɔːəɹ] and *another* [ənɔːəɹ].

11.7 *–ing* is /ɪn/.

11.8 /h/ is present.

11.9 Certain words which have /ʊ/ in RP and other accents may have /ʌ/ in Belfast speech: e.g. *wood* may be pronounced [wʊd] or [wʌd].

The recording

The main speaker is a middle-aged woman with a distinctive Belfast accent. The man who asks her questions is younger, and his accent is less broad. The woman talks about her past and about the fighting in the city.

... born in this house ... and still in it ... Raymond.

– You were born in this house?

I was born in this house, yes ... born ...

– So then you haven't lived in any other parts of Belfast, just this part?

5 Oh aye ... when I was about eight years of age my mother went down to the Ormeau Road to live, in Powerscourt Street. But then ... you

see my Uncle Tommy's lived here, and his wife died. And he got
married again, my mother come back to my granny. Her, er, mother,
and we've been there ever since again, that was in . . . during the . . . the
10 war, 1941 or something, we come back here, you know? So, counting
all round, we weren't so long on the Ormeau Road, really, you know.
I'd say about ten years, maybe twelve years, you know, no longer.

And then, when I was about s . . . sixteen or so, my grandmother got
me into a place called Carson's, a very high-class bakery shop.

15 – Was there any time when you yourself were sort of in danger
around there . . . when you had any . . . can you remember any time
when you were frightened?

I wouldn't say in danger, really, Raymond. We heard shooting and
all going on when we were in work, you know. Well, then they had a
20 gun battle . . . Belvoir . . . There was trouble down there really, you
know.

I think they had to close up for a couple of days, really, you know,
until it died down. But there was a fellow, one of the terrorists, was
shot on the roof, really, you know.

25 – Yeah, did you know any of the people that you knew in Inglis's who,
sort of, were shot, or anything like that? Or had, er . . .

No, only just round about that didn't work at Inglis's, really, you
know. The time the Republican, er . . . Remember the time they had a
. . . a bit of a feud between the two sides? Republican and the . . .

30 – The Provisionals?

Aye, it was the Provisionals and another . . . with Bernadette Devlin
was over . . . now there was . . . the initials, I just can't remember, the
initials, you know what I mean? Social something, you know . . . just
forget what the initials . . . Well, they had a bit of a go at each other,
35 you see, and there was shooting and . . . I remember one time when I
was in work at that time . . . and, erm, everybody was lying low at the
time, you know, I mean they were all disappearing. And I think half of
Inglis's disappeared for a few days. Even the security man
disappeared! They were all went . . . aye . . . and you know, and then
40 in a few days' time when it was all over they all come trotting back
again, you know? You don't know who . . . who was who, you know
what I mean?

– But were you never afraid, like, in the middle of winter going down
there . . . an . . . you walked down there, didn't you? It must have been
45 dark in the early mornings or evenings coming back. It's a dangerous

place to go now at night, isn't it? I mean some people wouldn't want to go there, you know.

Yes, I know, well . . . I never thought of danger, really, you know what I mean? It never struck me, you know?

50 – I mean, some people wouldn't walk in that area.

That's right, I know. I remember one day there was shooting all round over something, I don't know what it was. Oh, down all the streets there was shots getting fired here, there and everywhere. And I saw this yellow car sitting up Cromac Street, and a fellow over the
55 bonnet of it. I said that's very like Harry Short's, you know? Anyway, when I got up it was Harry Short, and all the shooting was going round him, and there was Harry, his car or something had went wrong and he was . . . says I, 'Harry, what are you doing here?' says I, 'you could be shot!' says I, 'you're . . . leaning over your bonnet fixing
60 your car!'

– What did he say to that?

He laughed hearty at the idea. He had to get a tow home by the RAC. Something went wrong where he couldn't start his car. He seemed to be . . . he didn't know that the shooting was going around him, he was
65 that interested in his car getting started.

Notes
1 *come* (l. 8, 10, 40) is the past tense of **come** (see p. 26).
   went (l. 39) is the past participle of **go** (see p. 26).
2 *says I* (l. 58), see p. 29.
3 *hearty* (l. 62), see p. 32.

12 Dublin

Although there are similarities between the English of the northern and southern parts of Ireland – /l/ is clear [l] in all positions throughout Ireland, for instance – the accents of Belfast and Dublin are very different. One reason for this is that there was no Scottish influence on the development of Dublin English. It is also worth noting that in the Republic of Ireland the highest prestige form of English, and the linguistic model to which many Irish people aspire, is not a British variety, but is that of Dublin (see Hickey 1999).

12.1 In some respects, the English of the Republic of Ireland, except that of the far north, resembles that of Bristol and other parts of south-west England. For instance, post-vocalic /ɹ/ (see p. 63) occurs, and the RP vowels /ɪə/, /ɛə/ and /ʊə/ are therefore absent.

Map 5.12

12.2 /a/, pronounced [a], and /ɑː/, pronounced [aː], are distinct and are distributed much as in RP. Note /a/ in *matter* (l. 16) and /ɑː/ in *after* (l. 1). In other parts of Ireland, however, /a/ and /ɑː/ may not be distinct.

12.3 /ɒ/ is pronounced [ɑ], cf. *lot* (l. 14) and /ɔː/ is pronounced [ɑː].

12.4 /aɪ/ has a back first element [ɑɪ ~ ɒɪ] which is nevertheless distinct from /ɔɪ/, e.g. *while* (l. 25).

12.5 /eɪ/ and /əʊ/ are mostly monophthongs or narrow diphthongs. The word-list speaker has fairly marked closing diphthongs in *bay*, *boat*, *pole*, *nose* (cf. *knows*, WL 39), *plate*, and *weight* (WL 8, 12, 29, 38, 40, 41), while the main speaker has [ei] in *Bray* (l. 5).

12.6 There is a strong tendency for /ʊ/ and /ʌ/ not to be distinct in strongly local Dublin accents, e.g. /ʊ/ in *government* (l. 6), but /ʌ/ does occur, particularly in more educated speech (see pp. 59–60).

12.7 /ɜː/ does not occur in lower-status accents. Instead, as in Scottish English (p. 103), words such as *firm* (l. 2) have /ɪɹ/, words such as *Germans* (l. 21) have /ɛɹ/, and words such as *work* (l. 2) have /ʊɹ/.

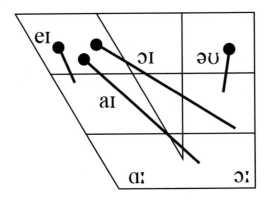

Figure 5.11
Phonetic qualities of certain Dublin vowels

12.8 Irish English has /a/ rather than /ɛ/ in *any* and *anyone* (l. 12).

12.9 /θ/ and /ð/ are often pronounced not as fricatives but as dental stops [t̪] and [d̪]. Before /ɹ/, /t/ and /d/ may also be pronounced as dental stops, so there may be no distinction /θɹ/ ~ /tɹ/, /ðɹ/ ~ /dɹ/, e.g. *true* ~ *through* [t̪ɹuː]. Note the occurrence of dental stops on the recording in *third* (l. 7), *north* (l. 10), and elsewhere.

12.10 /h/ is normally pronounced.

12.11 /p, t, k/ tend to be strongly aspirated, e.g. *it* (l. 33).

The recording

The main speaker on the CD is a Dublin man who is talking about experiences in Canada and the US, as well as early twentieth-century Irish history.

After a short while they got me into the painters' union, and I did clerical work. I was a trainee manager in Ireland for an English firm, *State Express 3335* cigarettes. My father was in the RAF and he was also in the First World's War, and I also lived in a British ex-service
5 house in Bray in County Wicklow. When I came down from Canada I was working for the Canadian government in a clerical position, I had two daughters and my wife was pregnant with the third, and the clerical job was paying $80 a week and the painting trade was paying $134 a week. So I went to night school and I had some Irish-Scotch
10 Americans, the mother from Glasgow, the father from the north of Ireland. Well, the Finnegan family taught me the greatest apprenticeship that anyone could ever got. I got a great apprenticeship off the Finnegans.

I played a lot of that Gaelic football, the Irish football, for years and I
15 was also a soccer player, and I'd been involved in many, many organizations. As a matter of fact we have a . . . an Easter Sunday commemoration mass here in the centre that I run on my own every year. And, er, they . . . the last two years now they done a video tape on it, about twenty-five minute tribute to the leaders of 1916. That's
20 when, you know, they rose up against England at the encouragement of the Germans. So, the thing was that a lot of people in Ireland during that period, there was a lock-out in Ireland in all factories and firms. They were trying to union organize and they just locked them out. And most of the children at that time had to be sent to England to
25 fellow union members to . . . to feed them, and keep them, while this happened. The First World's War started in 1914, and, er, England were giving a bonus to, er, anyone that volunteered. And the biggest mistake England made was Lloyd George sending, as they called

them, the Black and Tan. They were the veterans of the First World's
30 War who come back where unemployment, the economy was bad,
and half of these people ended up in jail. Well, what they did, instead
of letting the regular army quell that, they sent these people over in
1920, in a vigilante uniform, as they say it in Ireland.

Notes
1 *First World's War* (l. 4): more usually *First World War*.
2 *could ever got* (l. 12) = *could ever've got*.
3 *off* (l. 13) = Standard English *from*.
4 *they done* (l. 18) = Standard English *did*.
5 *Lloyd George* (l. 28): British Prime Minister from 1916 to 1922.
6 *come* (l. 30) = Standard English *came*.

13 Galway

The English of Galway is similar in most respects to that of Dublin,
although it has been much less heavily influenced by the English of
England, and exhibits more evidence of the effects of the influence of Irish
(the Celtic language also known as Gaelic or *Gaelge*), since in western
counties of Ireland Irish was widely spoken until relatively recent times.

13.1 /l/ is clear in all positions, e.g. in *pool* (WL 28), *Field* (l. 3).

13.2 /t/ is frequently **fricated** in syllable-final position, e.g. *pet, pat, put*
(WL 2, 3, 4), a salient feature of Irish pronunciation that has been
labelled the **Hiberno-English slit /t/** (Pandeli *et al.* 1997). The
speaker on the CD exhibits a very characteristic 'whistled'
articulation which can be heard in *pet, pot,* and *boat* (WL 2, 6, 12).
The slit /t/ can often sound very [s]-like, but direct comparison of
hat and *dance* (WL 21, 22) should serve to demonstrate the clear
difference between the two sounds. /d/ is also subject to this
process, e.g. *bird, bard, board* (WL 16, 17, 18).

Map 5.13

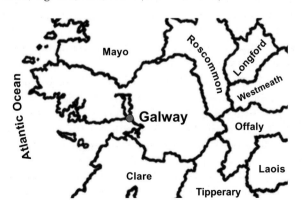

13.3 /a/ is pronounced with a noticeably closer vowel – [æ] – than that used by the Dublin speaker on the CD, e.g. in *bad* (l. 1), *flax* (l. 20), *hat* (WL 21). /ɑː/ is pronounced [aː] and can be quite distinct from /a/ – cf. the vowels of *half* and *father* (WL 24, 25) – but is close to [ɛ] in some words, e.g. *arch* (l. 8), *Armagh* (l. 16), *farmhouse* (l. 16), *aunt* (l. 17).

13.4 *Horse* is /haɹs/ (l. 3, 5).

13.5 /eɪ/ and /əʊ/ are monophthongs [ẹː] and [ọː], e.g. in *race* (l. 2).

13.6 There is no distinction between the vowels of *put* and *putt* (WL 4, 5), as both contain /ʊ/, but the words are nonetheless distinct on the word-list recording by virtue of the fact that the speaker uses very different realizations of /t/ (one fully fricated, the other with a stop + release sequence). Other examples are *months* (l. 12), *dust* (l. 14) and *coming* (l. 33).

13.7 *-ing* is /ɪn/, e.g. *racing* (l. 3).

Figure 5.12
Phonetic
qualities of
certain
Galway
vowels

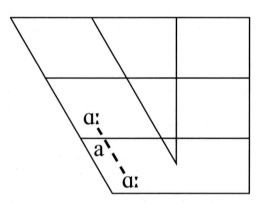

The recording

The speaker is a man in his sixties who has lived all his life in County Galway. He recalls the life of his father, who had been a policeman.

But he ha . . . he had two bad knocks. He had a very bad knock back in 1953 or '52. They used to have race . . . a race meeting in Clifden, out in Woods's Field. Pony racing, you know. There was a horse up . . . while everybody was at the races, anyway, there must have been
5 some kids messing around. But anyway, there was a horse being fed up there, so, er, what they did was tied a big sheet of galvanized onto the tail of the horse, and ran . . . it might have been tinkers, I don't know what the hell – and then chased him off down the arch. And my father was on duty at the time. And whatever way he tried to
10 stop the horse with his coa . . . with his coat. The horse swung around

and the sheet of galvanized caught him in the small of his back. And, jeez, he was ... he was for months in hospital down here. His back was gone. But anyway, he res ... resumed duty again, anyway. He got ... he got an old medal for that. And no dust. All they had was
15   bills.

[Talks of visiting relatives in Northern Ireland as a child]

Up in Armagh. Yeah, jeez, we loved it. Big farmhouse, you know. And then, let's say, my aunt had another big farm up behind us. And, you know, you used to run up the fields, you know, we'd be with the cattle, and killing pigs, and what not. And then there used to be
20   thrashing – you know, cutting the the flax. Flax was a big thing at that time, back in the Fif ... Forties and the Fifties and the Sixties.

I must tell you a good one now, and ... My ... my father, even though he was a sergeant in the Guards, we ... we ... we went from Clifden one time, to ... to, er, the North. Three of us. So the youngest, Brian,
25   stayed at home with mother. So it was a TD in Clifden, *Fine Gael* TD, he said he'd bring us to the station in ... in Dublin. So anyway, the three of us are in the back of the car. Before we were leaving, anyway. My father, he made us a big box of sandwiches, you know. And he says 'Don't eat them all now,' he says, 'because there's, er ... there's two big
30   salmon in the bottom of the box to bring up to the uncles.' And, like, it was a long day going up to Dublin and then up to ... up to Newry, and that time you'd stop at the ... at the border, and the RIC used to come in, the Special Branch coming in and checking who you are and had you any guns, or anything like that, because there was a lot of
35   trouble up there, even that ... that time. But it ... we were oblivious to all that, you never ... but we had the big box of sandwiches, we only ate a few of them. But as it transpired, anyway, we ... we had to hand over the box of sandwiches as a ... there was three bottles of poteen under the sandwiches [laughter] that he'd sent up to Peter and Patrick
40   and the boys.

[Asked if life was easier for children at the time under discussion]

Ar, it was. There was always an old few bob. Even when we were in ... reared back in Invern, like, you know, we'd be out in the curraghs, out fishing and everything like that, with the neigh ... the neighbours and everything, and, jeez, it was a fantastic life.

Notes
1   *bob* (l. 41) = a shilling, in pre-decimal currency. It is not confined to Ireland (it is used by the Liverpool speaker on the CD, for instance).
2   *curraghs* (l. 42) or *currachs* = small boats made on a frame of wickerwork (cf. *coracle*).

3   *Fine Gael* (l. 25, Irish 'tribe of the Gaels') = Ireland's second largest political party.
4   *galvanized* (l. 6) = a sheet of zinc-coated iron.
5   *jeez* (l. 16) = a mild religious oath (shortening of *Jesus*).
6   *poteen* (l. 38) (Irish *poitín*, 'little pot') = Irish whiskey, often distilled illicitly.
7   *RIC* (l. 32) = *Royal Irish Constabulary.*
8   *TD* (l. 25) stands for *Teachta Dála* (Irish 'deputy of the *Dáil*', the *Dáil* being the lower chamber of the Irish parliament), a role equivalent to that of MP (Member of Parliament) in the UK.
9   *tinkers* (l. 7) can refer to itinerant craftsmen, but here probably means Romani or travelling people more generally.

14 Devon

We conclude this section of the book with an examination of three traditional dialects of English which are very different from Standard English and RP (see p. 33). Varieties of this type are much less likely to be encountered by non-native learners, but are nevertheless of considerable interest.

The first traditional dialect is that of a rural area of Devon, in the south-west of England. The accent of this area is reasonably similar to that of Bristol, but there are some very clear differences.

Map 5.14

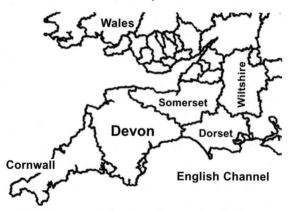

14.1   Devon lacks long mid diphthonging, so that /eɪ/ is [eː], e.g. *face* (l. 2), and /əʊ/ is [oː] or [uː], e.g. *local* (l. 3).

14.2   /uː/ is a front vowel approaching [yː] e.g. *improve* (l. 44).

14.3   At the beginning of words, /f, θ, s, ʃ/ may be /v, ð, z, ʒ/, e.g. *zy* /zaɪ/ (l. 17), *see* /ziː/ (l. 22), *thing* /ðɪŋ/ (l. 37).

14.4   As far as grammar is concerned, the following can be noted:

(a)   the present tense of **be** is *be* for all persons (see p. 35), e.g. *ponies be* (l. 28).

(b) *Isn't* and *wasn't* are pronounced *idden* [ɪdən] and *wadden* [wɒdən], e.g. (l. 14).

(c) The pronoun system is as discussed in Chapter 2, pp. 33–4. *He* is used for count nouns, including female animals: *he's a yow* (l. 9), *he got* (l. 5). The object form of *he* is *en*, as in *when you see en* (l. 22). Object forms may be used where subject forms would be expected: *us would call em* (l. 1–2), *whadd em* [= *what do they*] (l. 36). Subject forms may be used where object forms would be expected: *from they* (l. 33).

(d) *seed* = Standard English *saw* (l. 19); *tis* = *it's* (l. 29).

The recording

The speaker on the recording is a farmer in his fifties, talking about various aspects of farming and rural life.

Well now, there's some Scotch blackface sheep, that is. Us would call em possibly yows, or a ram, but that's Scotch blackface. That idden a local breeds. No. Now the local breeds, you see, there was the Widecombe whiteface. Now, Widecombe whiteface was a, is a curly-
5 coated sheep and he, he got, erm, he got horns, the ram carries horns, but the yow don't, and that was very much a local breed that was sold here at, er, Widecombe Fair each year. Then there's the greyface Dartmoor. Now, the greyface Dartmoor haven't got no horns, whether he's a ram, or whether he's a yow, a bigger sheep than the whiteface,
10 still big heavy curly coat, something like a Devon longwool, but this was brought in, these here Scotch sheep was brought down to, to Dartmoor ... oh beggar ... oh back, fifty years ago, I suppose or something as old as that. So, then, very much a breed here on the moors now. And there's a lot of fuzz there in the pictures, idden there?
15 Lot of fuzz, idden it? Eh? Yeah ... Beggar me, there idden a lot of grass there ... ain't enough grass to starve a rabbit, look like it!

That's a zy, yes, now that's a zy, and the interesting thing is that that is a manufactured snead. Now all zies got a snead. Snead's the handle! Snead's the handle. And years ago you used to cut a snead if you seed
20 the right-sized, the right-shaped stick, you see, and there is a Devonshire saying is 'when is the right time to cut a shovel-stick?' And the answer is 'when you see en!' So, so, you, it's the same with a snead. He got to have a right ... he got to have the right curve in it, see. No, no, generally halse, generally halse or ash, generally. Yeah, I
25 should think that's ash, but generally halse or ash. Because it tends to grow, but the right way with not too many natches in it. You don't want too many natches in it.

No, proper Dartmoor ponies be either a nice sort of dark, bit darker than chestnut, see, or black, but this here stuff, see, tis, that idden,
30 erm, that idden proper Dartmoor ponies. [indistinct] The National Park, they've got a sort of scheme going now, I believe, that with a little bit of sort of encouragement, trying to keep ... keep people to sort of stop breeding from they, see, but breed from the proper Dartmoor ponies, and ... and the Dartmoor ponies be hardier than
35 those ponies, see, and that's why years ago you didn't get half the trouble with these here Dartmoor – erm, whadd em call em? – erm, the Pony Protection Society, and that sort of thing, kicking up a shindig about the fact that the ponies be up a-starving on the moor, because the true Dartmoor pony, he was hardy, hardy, see? He could
40 weather the weather. And us used to get worst winters then than us do now, but he would, he would bide up on the moors. And he'd ... he'd dig away the snow, see, and get at the fuzz bushes and the heather and eat grass in under the fuzz bushes and he'd live happy, happy as [indistinct]. And then, course, when it got that riding ponies was all
45 the craze, they started breeding in this sort of stuff and trying to sort of improve em a bit. You get piebalds, cos they like ... the kiddies like the piebalds, and the screwballs, and that sort of ... but, no, that's ponies, yeah.

Notes

1   *yows* (l. 2) = *ewes.*
2   *fuzz* (l. 14) = *furze (gorse).*
3   *zy* (l. 17) = *scythe.*
4   *halse* (l. 24) = *hazel.*
5   *natch* (l. 26) = *notch.*
6   *shindig* (l. 38) = *fuss.*
7   *bide* (l. 41) = *stay.*

15 Northumberland

The speech of Northumberland is represented here by a traditional dialect speaker from Tyneside, the urban area which dominates this region. Northumbrian speech is similar in several respects to that of Scotland, owing both to the common ancestry of Northumbrian and Scottish dialects, and to prolonged cross-border contact between southern Scots and Northumbrians.

15.1 (a) As in other northern English (but not Scottish) accents, pairs of words like *put* and *putt* are not distinguished, /ʊ/ occurring in both (see p. 59).

Map 5.15

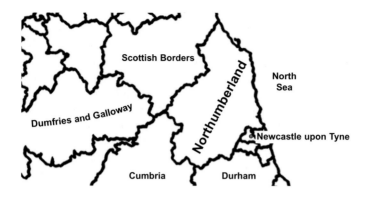

(b) The final vowel in words like *city* and *seedy* is /iː/; see p. 62.

(c) As has been seen, /eɪ/ and /əʊ/ are wide diphthongs in the south of England, narrow diphthongs further north, and monophthongs in northern Lancashire and Yorkshire. On Tyneside they may be either monophthongs [eː] and [oː], or centring diphthongs, [ɪə] and [ʊə]. But notice that *roll* (l. 61) has [ou]. Closing diphthongs of this sort are increasingly common among middle-class Tyneside speakers.

15.2 (a) Again as in other northern accents, words like *dance* and *daft* have /a/ (WL 22, 23).

(b) Words like *farm* and *car* have /ɑː/. This vowel may often be slightly rounded, or even [ɒː].

(c) Words which have /ɔː/ in RP are divided into two sets in traditional Tyneside speech:

   (i) Those which have -*al*- in the spelling have /aː/ e.g. *talking* (l. 59), *called* (l. 63), *all* (l. 56).

   (ii) Those which do not have -*al*- in the spelling have /ɔː/, as in RP (WL 18, 33, 44, 45; *morning* (l. 18)).

(d) Words which have /ɜː/ in RP have /ɔː/ in a broad Tyneside accent. Thus *first* (l. 11) and *shirt* (l. 34) are /fɔːst/ and /ʃɔːt/, and therefore homonyms of *forced* and *short*. This feature – the result of a backing process termed **burr retraction** (see 15.10, below) – is becoming less frequent in Tyneside speech, however.

By comparison with RP, then, the traditional accent of Tyneside lacks one vowel, /ɜː/, but has one extra, /aː/.

15.3 (a) Word final -*er(s)* or -*or(s)* is [ɐ(z)] (*tanner*, l. 5).

(b) /ɪə/ is [iɐ] (WL 14; *here* (l. 3)).

(c) /ʊə/ is [uɐ] (WL 42).

15.4   /aɪ/ is [ɛi] (*right* (l. 48)).

15.5   /l/ is clear in all environments (WL 27–31).

15.6   /h/ is generally present.

15.7   *-ing* is /ɪn/ (*shilling*, l. 2).

15.8   Between vowels, /p, t, k/ are usually glottalized. *city* may be transcribed ['sɪt͡ʔiː] or ['sɪd̠iː], where the /t/ is produced with (creaky) voicing throughout its length; *happy* (l. 30) is [hap͡ʔiː] (see p. 67).

15.9   (a) Just as in Scottish English, words which in RP have /aʊ/ may in Tyneside English have /uː/ e.g. *about* (l. 4), *out* (l. 7).

      (b) (i)   *knows* is /naːz/ (see l. 33 for contrast with *nose*).

          (ii)   *was*, when stressed, is /waz/, thus rhyming with *as*; *what* is /wat/ (rhyming with *that*); *who* (l. 67) is /we/.

          (iii)   Again, as in Scottish English, *no, do* (l. 29) and *nobody* (l. 67) have /e/.

          (iv)   As in Scotland, Tyneside pronunciations of *wrong* and *long* may have /a/ rather than /ɒ/, *long* (l. 61) is /laŋ/.

          (v)   *father* (l. 68) is ['faðɐ].

15.9   *Yourself* (l. 9) is [jəˈsɛl].

15.10 In parts of Northumberland and Durham /ɹ/ may be the uvular fricative [ʁ], the production of the sound involving the back of the tongue and the uvula, as per French or German, rather than the tip of the tongue and the alveolar ridge. The recorded speaker's /ɹ/ is variable. An example of uvular [ʁ] is found in *remember* (l. 4) (see p. 66) or *Durham* (l. 39). This feature, known as the 'Northumberland burr', is now recessive except among older people in rural areas of Northumberland, and is now virtually never heard in urban Tyneside.

The recording

The speaker is a man of about fifty who has lived almost all of his life in and around Newcastle. His accent is quite strong. He talks about the old days.

I'll tell you what, I often tell it at work. You know, they'd say to you, 'Hey, Jimmy, lend us a shilling, man'. 'What?' 'Lend us a shilling.' And I'd say to them, 'Come here a minute, I'll tell you.' I says, 'I can remember when I used to shove a bairn about in a pram for a tanner

5 a week. Lot of money, a tanner then a week.' And I says, 'I've been pushed for money ever since!' So they divven't come back. Put them

out the road. Wey lad, get away, go on. 'Aye,' he says, 'for a tanner. By, you can do a lot with a tanner. You can gan to the pictures, get yourself a penny fish and a haiporth of chips, by God, yeah, and
10 maybes a packet of Woodbines for tuppence, and a match in, for to get your first smoke.' Bah! I once ge . . . remember getting some Cock Robins . . . they cock-robinned me, I'll tell you. I was at Newburn Bridge . . . that's it, you can see Newburn, it's across there. And I was smoking away, faking, you know, instead of just going [smacks lips]
15 . . . swallowing down, you know, I was sick and turned dizzy. [laughter] I didn't know what hit us with these Cock Robins. Bah, but they were good ones.

This old woman says to me one morning, 'Sonny.' Sonny? Why, you never said 'sonny' them days, you know. She says, 'Would you like to
20 run a message for Mr Penn and for me?' I says, 'Yes, I will do.' She says, 'Go up to the shop and get him an ounce of tobacco.' 'Oh,' I says, 'thank you very much.' So I gans twaddling up the shop. When I gans back she give us thruppence – mind thruppence, you know, that's about forty . . . forty-two year ago, you know, Reg. Thruppence then
25 was a lot of money. I was there every day knocking at the door to see if she wanted any more messages! [laughter] Aye, thruppence. 'Wey lad, aye, I'm getting thruppence off that woman.' 'What for?' 'Wey, getting some baccy.' Wey, lad . . . Thruppence? What a lot of money that was. Oh dear me, oh, we used to do such things then, y . . .

30 We used to do some queer things then, but we were happy, man. Aye, we were happy. Once a rag man says to me, 'Hey, sonny!' 'What?' He says, 'Your hanky's hanging out.' Hanky? Wey, you never had a hanky then. You used to wipe your nose like that, you know. It was my shirt-tail hanging out of a hole in my pants! [laughter] 'Aye,' he
35 says, 'your hanky's hanging out.' Wey, you never had a hanky then. Bah! You used to gan to school. They used to line you up at school there. 'You want a pair of shoes, I think. You want a pair of shoes.' Wey, you never seen them, you know, it was just a day out from Durham County for somebody [indistinct] road. Them were the days,
40 huh.

Then I went from there . . . and there's a house up there just beside those two wireless poles. I went from there to there, and then I went and got married, and I went and lived there with Florrie, and, er, I was like a bit gypsy. I was in Blaydon first, and Greenside I was, in
45 Blaydon and Greenside. That's what the doctor says. He says, 'Jimmy, you've a little bit gypsy in you,' he says, 'we divven't know where you live.' Then I shifted from there to Crawcrook and from Crawcrook to Blaydon. Aye, that's right, aye. We sold the house at Crawcrook and I

went to Coventry, and when I come back I stopped with Florrie, and
50 then I got a council house into here. I've been in here about twelve
year, hin. Oh, if I gan out here I gan out with a stick, George, a stick
in a big box. That'd not be very long, would it? The box, about five
foot ten, that the measurement of us. When I get stiff, when I gan stiff
about five foot ten.

55 But you used to get summers, didn't you? Mind, you used to get the
winters and all, pet. Oh, dear me, ow the winters. You couldn't stand
the winters now. Youse lot couldn't stand it, could they? Course we
used to get the grub, you know. There was a fell . . . there was a fellow
at, er . . . when I'm talking about grub . . . he used to make leek
60 puddings. You've heard of leek puddings, you know? Right. But he
used to make them about a yard lang, see? Put the leek in, and roll the
leek up, see, just like, er, a sausage, see? And this fellow was sitting,
Japer Newton they called him, he had about four sons and a lass, like,
and he was sitting at the end of the table, like, all sitting with our
65 tongues hanging out, you know, George. He was sitting at the end
with a s . . . a big leek pudding. He says, er, 'Who wants the end?' So
nobody spoke, see? So he says again, 'Who wants the end, you
buggers!' Ted says, 'I'll have the end, father,' so he cut the bugger in
two. [laughter] Aye, he cut it in two, a great big leek pudding about a
70 yard lang, cut it in two! Dear me.

Notes
1 *us* (l. 2) = *me* (also l. 16).
2 *I says* (l. 3): see p. 29.
3 *bairn* (l. 4) = *child*, as in Scotland.
4 *tanner* (l. 5) = six pence, in pre-decimal currency (not limited to Tyneside).
5 *I've been pushed for money* (l. 5–6) = *I've been short of money*.
6 *divven't* (l. 6) = *didn't*, *don't*, or *doesn't*.
7 *wey* (l. 7, 26, etc.) = exclamation common on Tyneside (like *why* in other dialects).
8 *gan* (l. 8, 22) = *go*.
9 *haiporth* (l. 9) = contraction of *halfpennyworth* (not limited to Tyneside).
10 *maybes* (l. 10) = *maybe*.
11 *Woodbines* (l. 10): once a common and inexpensive brand of cigarettes.
12 *for to* (l. 10) = *to* (also found in Scottish and Irish English.)
13 *Bah!* (l. 11) exclamation, not limited to Tyneside.
14 Note the two pronunciations of *sonny* (l. 18), the first being an imitation of the woman's accent, RP or something approaching it, which the speaker clearly thinks was 'posh'.
15 *them* (l. 19) is used as demonstrative adjective.
16 *give* (l. 23) as past tense of **give** (see p. 27).

17 *thruppence* (l. 23) = *three pence* (not limited to Tyneside).

18 *baccy* (l. 28): colloquial form of *tobacco*.

19 *hanky* (l. 32): colloquial form of *handkerchief*.

20 *seen* (l. 38) as past tense of **see** (see p. 26).

21 *Durham County* (l. 39) = *Durham County Council*.

22 *them* (l. 39) as demonstrative pronoun (see p. 31).

23 *come* (l. 49) as past tense of **come** (see p. 26).

24 *twelve year* (l. 50–1) (see p. 32).

25 *pet* (l. 56): term of endearment much used on Tyneside. *Hin* (l. 51), short for *hinny*, has a similar meaning.

26 *youse* (l. 57) = *you* (cf. Liverpool, p. 101).

27 *grub* (l. 58): colloquialism for *food*.

28 *lass* (l. 63) = *girl* (used throughout Scotland and northern England).

29 *bugger* (l. 68): term of (often friendly) abuse, common in most parts of Britain, as well as a taboo word. In l. 68 *bugger* also refers to the leek pudding.

16 Lowland Scots

Of all the varieties of English spoken in the British Isles, Lowland Scots – sometimes also known as **Lallans** – is probably the most unlike Standard English and RP (note that there is dispute about whether Scots should, or can, be regarded as a variety of English at all; see, for instance, Kay 1993; McClure 1997). In this section we confine ourselves to the urban varieties spoken in Edinburgh and Glasgow. Rural varieties, which are spoken by a much smaller number of speakers, are more divergent still, and therefore provide even greater difficulties for foreign learners. Even native speakers of English often have serious trouble understanding local people in areas like Aberdeenshire.

As we have already seen, the vowel systems of all varieties of Scottish English are radically different from those of England (see section 9). The traditional dialects spoken by urban working-class Lowland Scots speakers on our recordings, however, have the following additional features:

16.1 /u/ may often occur in words which in RP have /aʊ/: *house*, for instance, may be /hus/ (pronounced [hʉs] or [hys]), and is often written as *hoose* or *hous* in Lowland Scots dialect literature. e.g. *round about* (l. 36).

16.2 Instead of having *coat* /kot/ and *cot ~ caught* /kɔt/, as described in section 9, working-class Edinburgh and Glasgow speakers may have *coat ~ cot* /kot/ and *caught* /kɔt/. That is, pairs like *socks* and *soaks*, *clock* and *cloak* may be identical, e.g. *brought* (l. 33).

16.3   A number of words which have /əʊ/ in RP and /o/ in Standard
Scottish English have /e/ in Lowland Scots. Thus *home* is /hem/,
bone is /ben/, *stone* is /sten/ and *no* is /ne/. This is often reflected in
Lowland Scots dialect writing by spellings such as *hame, bane, stane,
nae,* etc. The same vowel also occurs in *do* /de/ and *to* /te/.
Examples are *stones* /stenz/ (l. 30) and *no* /ne/ (l. 20).

16.4   Many words containing /a/ in Scottish English may instead have
/ɛ/: e.g. /ɛɹm/ *arm* or /gɹɛs/ *grass*. Examples on the CD are *harm*
(l. 41), *married* (l. 49).

16.5   Words such as *long* and *strong* have /a/ rather than /ɔ/ (cf. section
15), e.g. *wrong* /ɹaŋ/.

16.6   In the west of Scotland, including Glasgow, words such as *land*
and *hand* can have /ɔ/ rather than /a/, e.g. *handy* (l. 46).

16.7   Past participles of verbs typically end in /t/ where Standard
English would have /d/, e.g. *married* (l. 49), *feared* (l. 44).

The recording

There are two speakers on the CD. The first is an Edinburgh schoolboy
talking about gang fighting. The second is an older Glasgow woman
talking about her youth.

Speaker 1

Aw, it's the gangs. They just fight with knives and bottles and big
sticks and bricks. Takes place over at the big railway over there.
They've got a gang, they call it Young Niddrie Terror. Round here
they call it Young Bingham Cumbie, and that's how it starts . . . they
5 start fighting. And they fight with other yins, they fight with
Magdalene. That's away along the main road there. Magdalene's just
down that road. And they fight with the Northfields. And they go
away on buses, and go to a lot of other places to fight. [**asked how old
the gang members are**] Aw . . . about sixteen and that. [**asked why
10 boys join the gangs**] Don't know. [**asked if gang members live in
the speaker's neighbourhood**] Well, there's only one person that
lives round here, in this part, and the rest are . . . some of them live
away up the road there, and they're all round the scheme. Aw, there's
one of them, like, he . . . he takes a lot of them on, he's right strong,
15 aye. [**asked if he knows this person's name**] Well, they . . . they
have nicknames. I forget his name but . . . his nickname but . . . he is
strong. He fights with all these others . . . he takes about three on at a
time. Because he is big . . . aw, the police come rou . . . round just . . .
just wh . . . as it starts. See all the police at night, they're going round

20 the scheme, making sure there's no fights, and all the laddies just run
away when they see the police. Th . . . they run away and hide, till
they think it's safe. [**asked if the police always catch the gang
members**] Not always. They take them away down to the police
station. Well, if there's any serious injuries on anybody they'll get put
25 in the children's home or that. If they're, like, old enough they'll get
put there. [**asked if he knows anyone this has happened to**] No.
Only one person. That was Billy. He was caught just a couple of
nights or so ago. [**asked if any younger boys get involved in gang
fighting**] Some of them . . . Some. Well, they usually . . . there's wee-er
30 laddies than me that goes round there and start tossing stones at the
laddies round there. They usually get their . . . get battered fae them,
if they get caught.

Speaker 2

You don't know the way I was brought up. When I think on it now, I
think that it was kind of strict, because, er . . . it was an awful . . . oh,
35 a terrible lot of them living yet, and they're in the flats and they're all
round about, they've been meeting me with, 'Bella, you never . . . got
doing what we did.' And yet we were happy. We were quite happy in
the house with my mother and father. And we were sitting in that
room with the wee screens, keeking out at them all playing, in the
40 summer at nine o'clock. We were gone to our bed. Never done us
any harm. Now, I think it's right, to be like that. And we'd to ask my
father if . . . if we'd a boyfriend, we'd to ask my father. He would've
died. I went with *him* for a year afore we got engaged. And I went for
other five year . . . I was feared to tell my father. My mother said
45 'Belle, you need to tell your father'. I says 'You know what he is.' Cos
I was handy, I was the last lassie, you know, and I done everything.
She says, 'You'll need to tell him.' I says, 'No.' But Willy's mother . . .
he was, er, the youngest, and, ach, there were years atween the one
next to him, they were all married, and she was a widow, and . . . I
50 think they only got ten shillings then for a widow's pension. Oh, she
would be awful old the now. So we just made it up that we would
stay single like that the now. 'You help your mother, and I'll help
mine.' That the right way? And then he got to know. But my mother
saw . . .

Notes
1 *All* is /a/ (e.g. l. 13).
2 Niddrie, Bingham, Magdalene and Northfields are areas of Edinburgh.
   A *scheme* (l. 13) is a housing estate (housing scheme).

3   *yins* (l. 5) = *ones.*
    right strong (l. 14) = *very strong.*
    laddies (l. 20) = *boys, youths.*
    fae (l. 31) = *from.*
4   *think on* (l. 33) = *think about.*
    yet (l. 35) = *still.*
    wee (l. 39) = *small* (*wee-er* (l. 29) therefore = *smaller*).
    keeking (l. 39) = *peering.*
5   *we were gone to our bed* (l. 40) = *we had gone to bed.*
    done (l. 46) = *did.*
    we'd to (l. 42) = *we had to.*
    feared (l. 44) = *frightened.*
    lassie (l. 46) = *girl.*
    afore, atween (l. 43 and 48) = *before, between.*
    awful old the now (l. 51) = *very old now.*

Suggestions for using the book

In what follows we assume that readers have a copy of the CD available with this book, as being able to listen to the sound files associated with each variety of English described will greatly enhance the value of the book to the user.

The suggestions that we make here are aimed primarily at teachers, but individual readers working through the book on their own can also benefit from them. If such readers think of themselves as both teacher and student, they should be able to do most of the things that we suggest, doing the exercises and checking their understanding against our transcripts and analyses.

What is done with the book and recordings will depend among other things on whether readers are British or Irish, whether they are native speakers of English and, if not, what the standard of their English is, and the use to which they intend to put their new knowledge. For this reason alone we cannot say what should be done. Instead, we can suggest what might be done, based on our experience of using these materials with students of various backgrounds. Instructors can then select from our suggested exercises, modify them, and doubtless add to them, in whatever way they feel is appropriate to their particular teaching situation.

We suggest a number of activities: working with the main recordings; completing exercises based on a reading of the book; working with shorter additional recordings.

Working with the main recordings

Comprehension

Most students in our experience are attracted by the challenge of trying to understand the recordings on the CD. But we think it is important that the task set them should not be beyond their ability. Instructors will have to decide how much information and other help they need to give to particular groups of students. There is no need to use the recordings in the order in which they appear on the CD. As can be seen, we have made a geographical progression north through Britain, and then across to Ireland, and in general the accents tend to become increasingly different from RP.

This does not take into account, however, the broadness of accent of our speakers. For example, the Bristol speaker (whose accent is not especially strong) may be easier for some listeners to understand than the speaker from London (whose accent is quite strong), even though, phonologically at least, London speech is closer to RP than is Bristol speech. Almost certainly the most difficult recording for listeners will be the one of the Edinburgh schoolboy. Students can be given a recording, or part of the recording, and be required to:

(a) give the general sense of what they hear

(b) answer comprehension questions set by the instructor

(c) transcribe orthographically passages from the recording. This exercise compels students to concentrate hard and makes them recognize just what they understand and what they do not.

Analysis

In trying to understand what is said, presumably the learners must carry out some kind of informal analysis. But as an activity in itself, analysis probably best follows comprehension exercises.

(a) the instructor can ask for general observations on the accent (grammatical and lexical matters are perhaps most usefully treated separately)

(b) a check can be made to discover how general the noticed features are and whether they form part of a pattern

(c) the analysis arrived at in the class can be compared with ours. Where there are differences, the recording can be examined for further evidence. The stage at which the word list recordings are introduced into these activities will presumably depend on the nature and level of the students concerned, as well as on the time available.

(d) for some students it may be appropriate to attempt phonetic or phonological transcriptions of the recordings.

Exercises based on the text

We have set exercises on all of the chapters of the book which are intended to help readers to both check and reinforce their learning. Most of the answers will be found in the text, though we have added notes on one of the exercises (on p. 141).

Chapter 1

1. If English is not your native language, what causes you the greatest difficulty in understanding spoken British and Irish English? Try to relate your answer to what you have read in Chapter 1.

2. For another language that you know (possibly your own):

    (a) can you give examples of:

    - differences in pronunciation, grammar and vocabulary between people in different regions of a country where the language is spoken?

    - differences in pronunciation and vocabulary between people from different social classes?

    - forms of the language that are generally considered 'incorrect'?

    (b) • is there a city or region whose accent or dialect is regarded as somehow inferior?

    - is there a city or region whose accent or dialect is regarded as somehow superior?

    - on what basis are claims made for their inferiority or superiority? Do you think these claims are valid?

3. In the light of your answers to the previous question, compare the language you have taken your examples from with British English.

4. What would your response be to the suggestion that the following are 'wrong' in some way? (Refer to the IPA chart on p.ix if you are unsure which sounds are being referred to using phonemic transcription.)

spud	(for *potato*)
/aʊs/	(for *house*)
/ɪm/	(for *him*)
I never	(for *I didn't*)
I've seen him only yesterday	
There's two of us	
happen	(for *maybe, perhaps*)
cheers	(for *thank you*)

There are notes on this exercise at the end of the section (p. 141).

Chapter 2

1. Give an example of each of the following in non-standard English:
   (a) multiple negation with two negatives
   (b) multiple negation with three negatives
   (c) another form of negation found only in non-standard dialects
   (d) past tense and past participle with the same form (where this is not the case in Standard English)
   (e) present tense, past tense and past participle with the same form.

2. Where are you likely to hear native speakers in Britain saying?:
   (a) *He smoke a lot*
   (b) *I likes it*
   (c) *He dos (/duːz/) it all the time, do he?*
   (d) *I've nae had the chance*
   (e) *Where's thine?*
   (f) *Give 'n to we*
   (g) *Where's that pipe? Ah, there he is*
   (h) *Does he not want to go?*
   (i) *He gave it the girl*
   (j) *It needs altered*
   (k) *Give her that apples*

Chapter 3

1. Fill in the gaps in the following:
   (a) Clear [l] and dark [ɫ] are .... of the same phoneme. Some RP speakers use a .... in place of dark [ɫ] in some environments.
   (b) Some RP speakers make a distinction in pronunciation between *saw* and *sore*. They have one more vowel .... than other RP speakers. This is an example of .... variability.
   (c) When different speakers use a different series of phonemes in pronouncing the same word, we speak of .... variability. An example is the pronunciation of the word *lure*, which may be pronounced with or without /j/.
   (d) When different speakers pronounce the same phoneme in different ways in the same phonological environment, we speak of .... variability.

2. Name as many factors as you can think of which help to account for variability within RP.

3. Give the voiced equivalents of:

/p/	/ /	/θ/	/ /
/t/	/ /	/s/	/ /
/k/	/ /	/ʃ/	/ /
/f/	/ /	/tʃ/	/ /

4. How is the glottal stop used in RP?

5. When is /h/ likely to be dropped in RP?

6. Comment on the RP pronunciation of the nasals in the words *cotton*, *tenth*, and *emphatic*, and in the phrase *ten girls*.

7. Give examples of linking /ɹ/ and intrusive /ɹ/. For the latter, give examples of intrusive /ɹ/ occurring (a) across a word boundary and (b) within a word.

8. Fill in the gaps in the following:

    (a) There is an increasing tendency for the final syllable in words like *university* to have a vowel more like / / than / /.

    (b) In some unstressed syllables (such as the first syllable of *believe*) there is a growing tendency for / / to replaced by / /.

    (c) There is variability between /a/ and /ɑː/ in such words as .... and ....

    (d) Most words that were once pronounced with /ʊə/ (for example, ... and ....) are now pronounced with / / by most speakers.

    (e) There is a growing tendency for the vowel in words like (unstressed) *do* and *you* to become [ ].

9. Give examples of smoothing and levelling in RP.

Chapter 4

1. Fill in the gaps in the following:

    (a) Some speakers in the north of England do not distinguish between pairs of words like *look* and *luck*, having the vowel / / in both. However, other (particularly older) northern speakers have / / in *look* but / / in *luck*.

    (b) In northern English accents, the words *brass* and *plant* are pronounced with the vowel / /.

    (c) In most of the north of England, the final vowel of words like *city* is / /. Exceptions to this are L ...., H ...., and T ....

(d) Post-vocalic /ɹ/ survives in the .... of England, central ...., ..., and ....

(e) Scottish speakers make no distinction between *pull* and ...., or between *cot* and ....

(f) While /h/ is variably absent in most regional accents in England and Wales, it is retained in the .... of England, including the city of ....

2. Describe the use of [ʔ] in different parts of the British Isles.

3. In what ways does the pronunciation of the sound(s) represented in spelling by <ng> in the words *singer* and *breaking* vary in the British Isles?

4. Where are you likely to hear the word *beautiful* pronounced without /j/?

Chapter 5

Note: questions relate to the accent and dialect of the city or area referred to in the section title.

London

1. Fill in the gaps in the following:
    (a) The consonant in the middle of the word *water* may be realized as [   ], rather than as [t].
    (b) The initial sound in *thin* and the final sound in *breath* may be /   /, rather than /   /.
    (c) The second consonant in *bother* and the final consonant in *breathe* may be /   /, rather than /   /.
    (d) Initial /p, t, k/ are heavily ....

2. Describe the difference between the pronunciations of *paws* and *pause*.

3. In what phonological environments is /l/ realized as a vowel? What effect does this vocalization have on preceding vowels?

Norwich

1. What is noteworthy about the pronunciation of the word *few* in Norwich?

2. Give examples of words which are homophones in RP but which are distinct in Norwich English.

3. Give an example of homophones in Norwich speech which are distinct in RP.

4. How is <*-ing*> (in, for example, *walking*) pronounced?

Bristol

1. What is the 'Bristol /l/'?

2. In what obvious ways does the Bristol pronunciation of the word *bard* differ from that in RP?

3. Fill in the gaps in the following:

   (a) There is no /   / ~ /   / contrast in Bristol speech. The pronunciation of *daft* and *hat* illustrates this.

   (b) The vowel in the word *cup* is /   /. In Bristol there seems not to be a /   / ~ /   / contrast.

South Wales

1. In what way does /l/ differ from RP in South Wales accents?

2. Fill in the gaps in the following:

   (a) The vowels in words like *bird* exhibits ....

   (b) Between vowels, when the first vowel is stressed, consonants may be ....

   (c) /a/ and /ɑː/ are distributed largely as in the north of England, but are normally distinguished by .... alone.

3. In what ways is Welsh English influenced by Welsh?

West Midlands

1. In which ways can the accent be classified as northern, and in which ways does it resemble a southern accent?

2. What is the vowel in the word *one*?

3. Indicate the West Midlands pronunciations of the following vowels on a vowel quadrilateral chart: /ɪ, iː, uː, aɪ, eɪ, əʊ/.

Leicester

1. What are the key differences between East Midlands accents and West Midlands ones?

2. Give an example of homophones in a Leicester accent which are distinct in RP.

3. Fill in the gaps in the following: /l/ is .... in syllable-initial position in this accent, as in *leaf*, but is usually ....
    .... or can even be .... in syllable-final position, as in *feel*.

Bradford

1. Fill in the gaps in the following:
    (a) The words *gas* and *grass* have the same vowel, which is /   /.
    (b) The words *rush* and *push* have the same vowel, which is /   /.
    (c) The final vowel in words like *city* is /   /.
2. Describe the realizations of /eɪ/ and /əʊ/.
3. In what way can a Yorkshire accent generally be distinguished from a Lancashire accent?
4. Give a phonemic transcription of *Bradford* as pronounced by someone with a West Yorkshire accent.

Liverpool

1. In what ways is the Liverpool accent northern? In which way does it resemble southern English accents?
2. In a description of Liverpool speech, what is the significance of pairs of words like *fare* and *fur*?
3. Fill in the gaps in the following:
    (a) /p, t, k/ are heavily .... and in final position may even be realized as ....
    (b) /ɹ/ is usually a ....
    (c) The word *thing* can be transcribed [   ].
    (d) .... is present throughout Liverpool speech giving it a distinctive quality.

Edinburgh

1. List the vowels of Scottish English as they are described in this book.
2. Assign each of the words in the word list to one of the vowels you have listed.
3. Comment on the following pairs of words: *witch~which, pull~pool, tide~tied*.

Aberdeen

1. What is special about the way in which the first consonant is traditionally pronounced in words like *where, what* and *when*?

2. Fill in the gaps in the following:

   (a) /p, t, k/ in word-initial position are only very lightly .... Their voiced counterparts, / /, / / and / /, are ...., meaning that voicing starts before the stop closure is released.

   (b) As in other Scottish accents there is no RP-like / /~/ / distinction in the open vowels, but the vowel of words like *chap* or *that* is much further .... than is typical for, say, Edinburgh speech.

   (c) The vowels of the words *fir, fern* and *fur* have not undergone ...., as in RP, but retain their original qualities / /, / / and / /, respectively.

Belfast

1. In what ways is the Belfast vowel system different from that of Edinburgh?

2. What determines the length of vowels?

3. What consonant may be lost between vowels? Give an example of a word in which this may happen.

4. As in Scottish English, which consonant is present, although it is variably absent in most urban accents of England and Wales?

Dublin

1. Fill in the gaps in the following:

   (a) As in Wales and in Belfast, /l/ is always ....

   (b) As in Liverpool English, /p, t, k/ tend to be strongly ....

   (c) The fricatives / / and / / are often pronounced as dental stops.

   (d) As in Scotland, Belfast and south-west England, ... occurs.

2. Comment on /a/ and /ɑː/ in Dublin English.

Galway

1. What is the Hiberno-English slit /t/?

2. Fill in the gaps in the following:

(a) In Galway English, / / and / / tend not to be distinct, and words like *brother* have / /.

(b) The vowel / / in words like *mad, happy*, etc. is [   ], and is therefore close to the extent that it can often sound like / /, as in *bed*.

(c) As in the north of England, / / and / / are not distinct, such that *cud* and .... are homophones.

Devon

1. Which voiceless RP consonants may be voiced in Devon speech? In what linguistic environment?

2. In which way do the vowels in *lace* and *soak* differ from their RP equivalents?

3. Fill in the gaps in the following:

   (a) *Isn't* and *wasn't* are pronounced [   ] and [   ].

   (b) The present tense of the verb **to be** for all persons is ....

   (c) *Tis* [tɪz] is the equivalent of Standard English ....

Northumberland

1. Fill in the gaps in the following:

   The accent is northern in that the vowel [   ] occurs in both *put* and *putt*, and [   ] occurs in both *daft* and *dance*, but resembles southern accents in that ....

2. Older forms of the traditional accent of Tyneside lack one vowel, by comparison with RP. What is it?

3. What is significant about the pronunciation of /l/?

Lowland Scots

1. Transcribe the following words as they would be pronounced in a broad Lowland Scots accent:

round	[ ]
harm	[ ]
wrong	[ ]
land	[ ]
do	[ ]
stone	[ ]

Notes to exercise 4, Chapter 1 _____

All are perfectly appropriate (and so not 'wrong') in the right circumstances: *spud* is colloquial Standard English; the absence of /h/ is a common feature of regional accents, including that of London (Chapter 5); in unstressed syllables /h/ is also frequently absent in RP (Chapter 3); *I never* is a feature of regional dialects (Chapter 2); the co-occurrence of present perfect and definite past time reference seems to be on the increase in Standard English (Chapter 1); *there* plus singular verb with plural complement is quite usual in informal Standard English; *happen* meaning *maybe* or *perhaps* is found in northern dialects (see Chapter 5); *cheers* is used very frequently to mean *thank you* in informal Standard English, as *Cheers for bringing the cakes*.

Using the test passages _____

There are thirteen additional recordings to be found on the CD. These are provided to allow readers to test their ability to recognize and understand regional speech, and should be left until all the transcribed and annotated recordings have been worked through.

The first ten of the additional recordings, which are very brief, exemplify the accents found in some of the main recordings. Students may be asked to identify each accent and to justify their choice. They can also be asked to make transcriptions.

Test passages 11 to 13 are rather longer. These represent accents which, though they are not dealt with in Chapter 5, can be identified using the information provided in Chapter 4. It is suggested that the first step should be to listen to a recording once or twice to get the general sense of what is being said. Students can then listen again, checking what they hear against the features found in Table 4.2 (it should be noted that individual recordings may not contain examples which permit decisions with respect to all of the features). This should in itself be sufficient to identify the approximate source of each recording, but other features of pronunciation treated in Chapter 4 may be used to confirm the identification. There are a number of dialectal features which are also worth noting. It is a useful exercise to compare each accent with the one(s) treated in Chapter 5 that seem closest to it. As with previous recordings, students can be asked to provide orthographic transcriptions in order that they may discover for themselves precisely how much they do and do not understand.

If you listen to these thirteen tracks in order, you will hear first of all the ten short recordings from the varieties exemplified in Chapter 5. This is then followed by the longer recordings of the three new varieties to be identified. Notes on the three new varieties are given on the next page.

Notes on test passages 11–13 _____

The following brief notes are not exhaustive, as we have concentrated on the main identifying features only, in each case.

Test passage 11

This displays the following features: the vowel in *blood*, *up*, etc. is /ʊ/ not /ʌ/; the first vowel in *basket* is /a/ not /ɑː/; the final vowel in words like *journeys* is /ɪ/; /h/ is variably absent; *bring* is /bɹɪŋg/; there is no /ɹ/ in words like *poor*; a diphthongal pronunciation of /eɪ/ is found in *train*, *table*, *strange*, etc.; *one* is /wɒn/ (see p. 60). This is sufficient to identify the speaker as being from the north-west Midlands (she is in fact from Manchester). The accent in Chapter 5 probably closest to this is that of Bradford; note in particular that in both accents /ɹ/ is a tap [r], /t/ is often realized as glottal stop [ʔ], and /aɪ/ is realized as [ae]. There are also some similarities with Liverpool and the West Midlands. Note the use in the north of Britain of *right* as an intensifier (see p. 130): *right high up = very high up*.

Test passage 12

/ʌ/ (realized as [ə]) is found in words like *bucket*; the vowel in words like *plant* is /ɑː/; the final vowel in *plenty*, *properly*, etc. is /iː/; /ɹ/ is not present in words like *heart*; the vowel in *make* is /eː/, while in *day* it is /eɪ/ (see p. 85); /h/ is variably absent. This is sufficient to identify the accent as Welsh. In fact it is a north Welsh accent, the speaker having been born in Bangor but now living on the Isle of Anglesey. The accent closest to this in Chapter 5 is, not surprisingly, that of south Wales. Note the following shared features: doubling (or **gemination**) of the consonant in *open*, *apple*, *adding*; /ɹ/ as a tap; the vocalic nature of the sound which comes after /n/ in *manure*. In contrast to south Wales, however, the north Wales recording does not exhibit lip-rounding on the vowel in words like *first*; /l/ is not clear in all environments; and /t/ is strongly aspirated.

Test passage 13

The vowel in words like *son* is /ʊ/; the final vowel in *wealthy* and *army* is /ɪ/; /h/ is variably absent, e.g. *home*, *husband*; *anything* and *nothing* end with /ŋg/; the first vowel in *Daisy* is a diphthongal realization of /eɪ/. This is sufficient to identify the speaker as being from the north-west Midlands, as in the second of these recordings. In this case the speaker is from Derby. Nevertheless, it is possible to distinguish between the two accents. The diphthongs /eɪ/ and /əʊ/ are wider in Derby than in Manchester (see p. 68); /ɹ/ is not a tap in Derby (see p. 65). The intonation is also different; the Manchester intonation is somewhat like that of Merseyside; the Derby intonation is more similar to that of the West Midlands. These two examples will serve to remind the reader that it is possible to make finer and finer distinctions between accents of increasingly restricted areas. Note the non-standard *spotless clean.*

Further reading

For a detailed and up-to-date description of RP, the reader is referred to A. Cruttenden, *Gimson's Pronunciation of English* (6th edition, Arnold, 2001). More general accounts of the phonology of RP (and comparisons of RP with the other reference accents General American and Scottish Standard English) are given in A.M.S. McMahon, *An Introduction to English Phonology* (Edinburgh University Press, 2002) and P. Carr, *English Phonetics and Phonology: An Introduction* (Blackwell, 1999).

For an account of historical changes in English, see C. Barber, *The English Language: A Historical Introduction* (2nd edition, Cambridge University Press, 2000), A.C. Baugh and T. Cable, *A History of the English Language* (5th edition, Routledge, 2002) or B.A. Fennell, *A History of English: A Sociolinguistic Approach* (Blackwell, 2001). D. Britain (ed.), *Language in the British Isles* (2nd edition, Cambridge University Press, 2005) and G. Price (ed.), *Languages in Britain and Ireland* (Blackwell, 2000) have entries on the history of English in the British Isles as well as chapters on other languages currently and/or formerly used in the UK and Ireland.

To gain an appreciation of how normal conversational English differs from the careful style of English often most familiar to students, G. Brown, *Listening to Spoken English* (2nd edition, Longman, 1990), P. Roach, *English Phonetics and Phonology: A Practical Course* (3rd edition, Cambridge University Press, 2000), J. Kenworthy, *The Pronunciation of English: A Workbook* (Arnold, 2000), or M.L.G. Lecumberri and J.A. Maidment, *English Transcription Course* (Arnold, 2000) are useful.

J.C. Wells, *Accents of English* (Cambridge University Press, 1982) provides a wealth of detail on British Isles accents, as does P. Foulkes and G.J. Docherty, *Urban Voices: Accent Studies in the British Isles* (Arnold, 1999), though the latter is quite technical in places. Both these books come with accompanying sound recordings on cassette tape or CD. J. Milroy and L. Milroy (eds), *Real English: The Grammar of English Dialects in the British Isles* (Longman, 1993) and P. Trudgill and J.K. Chambers (eds), *Dialects of English: Studies in Grammatical Variation* (Longman, 1991) deal with variation in English grammar. P. Trudgill, *Dialects* (Routledge, 1994), M. Wakelin, *English*

Dialects: An Introduction (Athlone Press, 1977), M. Wakelin, *Discovering English Dialects* (Shire Publications, 1999), and P. Trudgill, *The Dialects of England* (2nd edition, Blackwell 1999) give information on both modern and traditional dialects and accents.

B. Kortmann and E.W. Schneider (with K. Burridge, R. Mesthrie and C. Upton), *A Handbook of Varieties of English: A Multimedia Reference Tool* (Mouton de Gruyter, 2005) combines printed and electronic information on the grammars and phonologies of varieties of English around the world, and includes entries on major varieties of English in the British Isles.

Several academic journals are dedicated to the study of the English language in its various forms, including *English World-Wide*, *English Language & Linguistics*, *World Englishes*, and *English Today*.

There is an increasing amount of information available online, though this should always be approached with care, as it is highly variable in quality, relevance and accuracy. A wide range of electronic resources dealing with varieties of English in the British Isles and around the world, many of which feature sound files and video clips, can be accessed via **http://www.abdn.ac.uk/langling/resources/**

References

Altendorf, Ulrike (2003). *Estuary English: Levelling at the Interface of RP and South-eastern British English*. Tübingen: Gunter Narr Verlag.

Bauer, Laurie (2002). *An Introduction to International Varieties of English*. Edinburgh: Edinburgh University Press.

Brown, Gillian (1990). *Listening to Spoken English*, 2nd edn. London: Longman.

Cruttenden, Alan (1995). Rises in English. In Windsor Lewis, J. (ed.), *Studies in General and English Phonetics: Essays in Honour of Professor J.D. O'Connor*. London: Routledge. pp. 155–73.

Cruttenden, Alan (1997). *Intonation*, 2nd edn. Cambridge: Cambridge University Press.

Cruttenden, Alan (2001). *Gimson's Pronunciation of English*, 6th edn. London: Arnold.

Dailey-O'Cain, Jennifer (2000). The sociolinguistic distribution of and attitudes toward focuser *like* and quotative *like*. *Journal of Sociolinguistics* 4(1): 60–80.

Docherty, Gerard J. and Watt, Dominic (2001). Chain shifts. In Mesthrie, Rajend (ed.), *The Pergamon Concise Encyclopedia of Sociolinguistics*. Amsterdam: Elsevier Science. pp. 303–7.

Fabricius, Anne (2002). Ongoing change in modern RP: evidence for the disappearing stigma of T-glottalling. *English World-Wide* 23(1): 115–36.

Fletcher, Janet, Grabe, Esther and Warren, Paul (2005). Intonational variation in four dialects of English: the high rising tune. In Jun, Sun-Ah (ed.), *Prosodic Typology and Transcription: A Unified Approach*. Oxford: Oxford University Press. pp. 390–409.

Foulkes, Paul (1998). English [r]-sandhi: a sociolinguistic perspective. *Leeds Working Papers in Linguistics and Phonetics* 6: 18–39.

Foulkes, Paul and Docherty, Gerard J. (1999). *Urban Voices: Accent Studies in the British Isles* (with audio CD). London: Arnold.

Foulkes, Paul and Docherty, Gerard J. (2000). Another chapter in the story of /r/: 'labiodental' variants in British English. *Journal of Sociolinguistics* 4(1): 30–59.

Foulkes, Paul and Docherty, Gerard J. (2005). Phonological variation in the English of England. In Britain, D. (ed.). *Language in the British Isles*, 2nd edn. Cambridge: Cambridge University Press.

Gick, Bryan (2002). The American intrusive *l*. *American Speech* 77(2): 167–83.

Giles, Howard (1970). Evaluative reactions to accents. *Educational Review* 22: 211–27.

Giles, Howard, Baker, Susan and Fielding, Guy (1975). Communication length as a behavioural index of accent prejudice. *International Journal of the Sociology of Language* 6: 73–81.

Gimson, A.C. (1988). *An Introduction to the Pronunciation of English*, 4th edn. London: Arnold.

Hickey, Raymond (1999). Dublin English: current changes and their motivation. In Foulkes, Paul and Docherty, Gerard J. (eds), *Urban Voices: Accent Studies in the British Isles*. London: Arnold. pp. 265–81.

Johnson, Wyn and Britain, David (2005). L vocalization as a natural phenomenon. To appear in *Language Sciences* 27.

Jones, Mark J. (2002). The origin of Definite Article Reduction in northern English dialects: evidence from dialect allomorphy. *English Language and Linguistics* 6: 325–45.

Kay, Billy (1993). *Scots: The Mither Tongue*, revised edn. Darvel: Alloway Publishing.

Ladefoged, Peter and Maddieson, Ian (1996). *The Sounds of the World's Languages*. Oxford: Blackwell.

Mathisen, A.G. (1999). Sandwell, West Midlands: ambiguous perspectives on gender patterns and models of change. In Foulkes, P. and Docherty, G.J. (eds), *Urban Voices: Accent Studies in the British Isles*. London: Arnold. pp. 107–23.

McClure, J. Derrick (1997). *Why Scots Matters*. Edinburgh: Saltire Publications.

McClure, J. Derrick (2002). *Doric: The Dialect of North-East Scotland*. Amsterdam: John Benjamins.

McRae, Sandra (2000). The demonstrative pronouns in the North-East: an introductory discussion. *Scottish Language* 19: 66–82.

Milroy, James (2001). Received Pronunciation: who 'receives' it and how long will it be 'received'? *Studia Anglica Posnaniensia* 36: 15–33.

Milroy, James and Milroy, Lesley (1993, eds), *Real English: The Grammar of English Dialects in the British Isles*. London: Longman.

Palmer, Frank R. (1988). *The English Verb*, 2nd edn. London: Longman.

Pandeli, Helen, Eska, J.F., Ball, Martin and Rahilly, Joan (1997). Problems of phonetic transcription: the case of the Hiberno-English slit-t. *Journal of the International Phonetic Association* 27: 65–75.

Petyt, K.M. (1977). 'Dialect' and 'accent' in the Industrial West Riding. Unpublished PhD thesis, University of Reading.

Przedlacka, Joanna (2002). *Estuary English? A Sociophonetic Study of Teenage Speech in the Home Counties*. Oxford: Peter Lang.

Rahilly, Joan (1997). Aspects of prosody in Hiberno-English: the case of Belfast. In Kallen, Jeffrey (ed.), *Focus on Ireland* (Varieties of English Around the World G21). Amsterdam: John Benjamins. pp. 109–32.

Rosewarne, David (1984). Estuary English. *Times Educational Supplement,* 19 October 1984.

Scobbie, James, Hewlett, Nigel and Turk, Alice (1999). Standard English in Edinburgh and Glasgow: the Scottish vowel length rule revealed. In Foulkes, Paul and Docherty, Gerard J. (eds), *Urban Voices: Accent Studies in the British Isles*. London: Arnold. pp. 230–45.

Stockwell, Peter (2002). *Sociolinguistics: A Resource Book for Students*. London: Routledge.

Stuart-Smith, Jane (2003). The phonology of modern urban Scots. In Corbett, John, McClure, J. Derrick, and Stuart-Smith, Jane (eds). *The Edinburgh Companion to Scots*. Edinburgh: Edinburgh University Press. pp. 110–37.

Tagliamonte, Sali and Hudson, Rachel (1999). *Be like* et al beyond America: the quotative system in British and Canadian youth. *Journal of Sociolinguistics* 3(2): 147–72.

Tollfree, Laura (1999). South-east London English: discrete versus continuous modelling of consonantal reduction. In Foulkes, Paul and Docherty, Gerard J. (eds), *Urban Voices: Accent Studies in the British Isles*. London: Arnold. pp. 163–84.

Torgersen, Eivind Nessa (2002). Phonological distribution of the FOOT vowel, /ʊ/, in young people's speech in south-eastern British English. *University of Reading Working Papers in Linguistics* 6: 25–38.

Trudgill, Peter (1974). *The Social Differentiation of English in Norwich*. Cambridge: Cambridge University Press.

Trudgill, Peter (2002). *Sociolinguistic Variation and Change*. Edinburgh: Edinburgh University Press.

Wakelin, Martyn (1977). *English Dialects: An Introduction*, 2nd edn. London: Athlone.

Walters, J. Roderick (2001). English in Wales and a Valleys accent. *World Englishes* 20(3): 285–304.

Walters, J. Roderick (2003). On the intonation of a South Wales Valleys accent. *Journal of the International Phonetic Association* 33(2): 211–38.

Watt, Dominic and Tillotson, Jennifer (2001). A spectrographic analysis of vowel fronting in Bradford English. *English World-Wide* 22(2): 269–302.

Wells, John C. (1982). *Accents of English* (3 vols). Cambridge: Cambridge University Press.

Wells, John C. (1984). The cockneyfication of RP? In Melchers, Gunnel and Johannesson, Nils-Lennart (eds), *Non-Standard Varieties of Language*. Stockholm: Almqvist & Wiksell. pp. 198–205.

Index

Note: Because Scottish and Irish vowel phonemes cannot be compared directly on a one-to-one basis with Anglo-English equivalents, they have not been included in the index. The reader is referred to sections 9, 10, 11, 12, 13 and 16 of Chapter 5.